Portraits of Exceptional African American Scientists

by

Doris Hunter Metcalf

illustrated by Marilynn G. Barr

Cover by Ted Warren

ISBN No. 0-86653-800-3

Printing No. 98765432

Good Apple
1204 Buchanan St., Box 299
Carthage, IL 62321-0299

Paramount Publishing

Table of Contents

Dedication

This book is dedicated to my husband Weston Metcalf, whose help with the household chores made it possible for me to complete this book on time.

Introduction

Portraits of Exceptional African American Scientists is a resource book of biographical information and related activity sheets designed to

- supplement social studies textbook information.
- develop an awareness of and a pride in the accomplishments and contributions of African American scientists and inventors.
- develop logical and critical thinking skills.
- develop and enhance skills in reading comprehension, writing, and research.
- develop and exercise creative thinking and creative problem-solving skills.

The activity sheets following the biographical information sheets consist of word searches, puzzles, games, and other high-interest learning activities. The activity pages can be used by the entire class as independent study projects or as meaningful learning center activities for those students who finish classroom assignments early. There are also eight appendix pages. These pages include a list of super science books and kits, magic science tricks, and other useful activity pages.

These pages may be used in various ways. The teacher is encouraged to use his or her own creative abilities in determining their use for the class. A study of the lives of these exceptional African American scientists can inspire students to set and achieve exceptional goals for themselves. It can help them to realize that success can be theirs if they are willing to study, work hard, and become committed to achieving success.

Most of the scientists are from the past. A few are contemporary, but all have one thing in common: they have all overcome obstacles to make significant contributions to the field of science. All children need to know about these important people and their significant contributions. African American children especially need to know about them so they might serve as role models and give them reasons to achieve.

Madam C.J. Walker
(Sarah Breedlove)

Madam C.J. Walker
(Sarah Breedlove)
(1867-1919)
Cosmetic Developer and Businesswoman

Madam C.J. Walker was born poor, but she died a millionaire. Her hair and cosmetic products made her one of the most successful businesswomen of the early twentieth century. Her success began when she discovered a formula to be used with a hot comb to straighten the hair. She sold her products through door-to-door salesmanship, trained agents, demonstrations, and lectures.

Madam Walker was born Sarah Breedlove to ex-slave parents in Delta, Louisiana. She was orphaned at the age of seven and was reared by her married sister. She married at the age of fourteen. By the time she was twenty years old, her husband had died and left her a widow with a small child. Determined that her daughter would have a good education, she moved to St. Louis where she married Charles Walker. She took the name Madam C.J. Walker to advertise her hair styling and cosmetic formulas. In 1910 she traveled to Indianapolis and began to manufacture her hair formula. She expanded her business by adding a line of toiletries and beauty products. She established many beauty schools across the nation and became the first African American woman millionaire.

She invested some of her money in real estate. She built for herself a lavish home at Irvington-on-Hudson, designed by the African American architect Vertner Tandy.

Not all of her money was spent on herself. She donated money to charities and African American colleges such as Tuskegee Institute and Bethune Cookman College. In her will she left much of her wealth to her daughter, but she also stipulated that two-thirds of the profits from her company were to be donated to charitable organizations.

Today, American as well as foreign students train at Walker beauty schools throughout the United States.

Beautiful Design

There is an old saying that "beauty is in the eye of the beholder." This means that each person has his or her own idea of what is beautiful. Use scissors and markers or crayons to cut out and color the shapes on this page. Then glue them on a colorful sheet of construction paper to make a beautiful design. Compare your beautiful design with those of your classmates. How different are they? With your teacher's permission, display your beautiful design in the classroom for all to see.

Dream Cream

Each year millions of dollars are spent on beauty products. You are a chemist for the Makeup Beauty Corporation. Your job is to develop a new beauty product. Answer the questions below about your new product.

1. What is the name of your product? ______________________________

   ____

2. How will it be used? ______________________________

   ____

3. What will it do for the person who uses it? ______________________________

   ____

4. What is the price of your product? ______________________________

   ____

5. How will your product be packaged (tube, box, jar, etc.)? ______________________________

   ____

Draw a picture of your product and write a television commercial to advertise it. Use the back of this sheet or another sheet of paper if you need more space.

In the Bright Lights

Madam C.J. Walker was born Sarah Breedlove. She later changed her name to Madam C.J. Walker to advertise her beauty products. Movie stars, singers, and other entertainers often change their names for many different reasons.

You have become a famous person. What are you famous for? Are you a famous actor/actress, singer, dancer?

____

____

____

You have changed your name. What is your new name? ____________________

Famous people sometimes use fancy handwriting when they sign autographs. Write your real name in a fancy way.

Write your new name in a fancy way.

You are performing at the Great Performance Theater. Announce your performance on the marquee below.

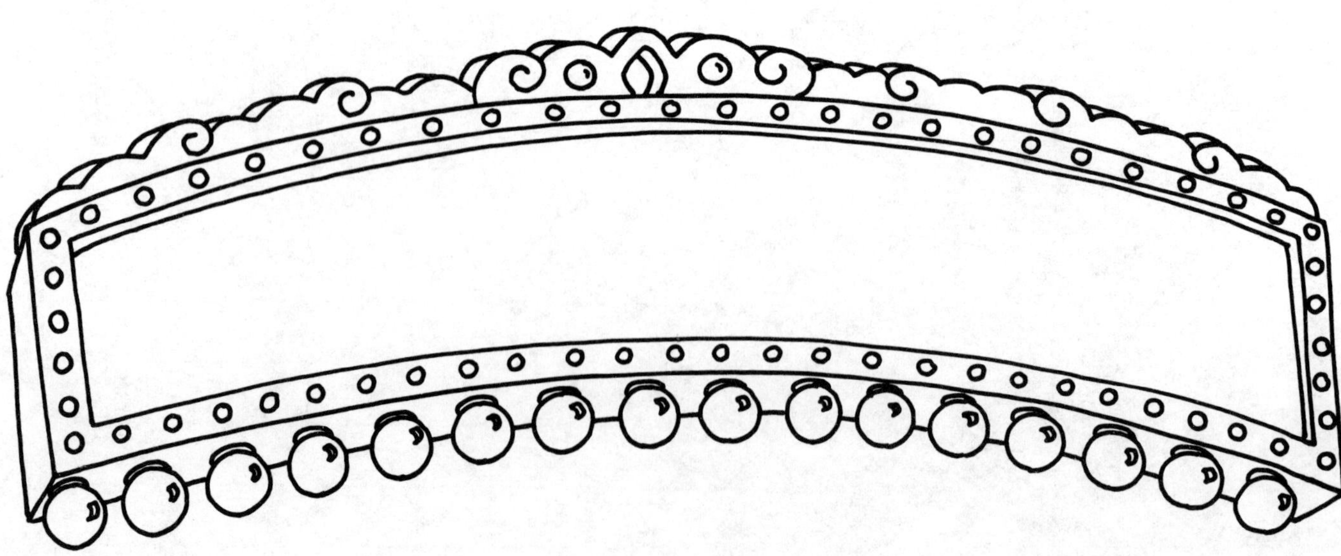

Makeup – Make-Over

Cosmetics and makeup are nothing new. Makeup has been around for thousands of years. Evidence from archaeologists shows that ancient Egyptians used perfumes and anointing oils as early as 400 B.C. In some cultures men as well as women wear makeup. The Food and Drug Administration classifies cosmetics as anything that is used to clean, change, or make the body more attractive.

On the cosmetic list below, place a check beside any cosmetic product that you have used this week.

1. perfume
2. cologne
3. sachet
4. face powder
5. rouge
6. lipstick
7. mouthwash
8. talcum powder
9. suntan lotion
10. deodorant
11. hair straightener
12. body or hand lotion
13. shampoo
14. nail polish
15. nail polish remover
16. hair remover
17. shaving lotion
18. hair coloring
19. mascara
20. bubble bath
21. foot powder
22. hair spray
23. hair oil
24. toothpaste

An alien from space is visiting you. There are no cosmetics on his planet. Select five cosmetic words from the list and write an explanation of what they are and how they are used. Keep it simple. Remember that the alien has never seen or used any cosmetics before.

______________________ ______________________________________

____

______________________ ______________________________________

____

______________________ ______________________________________

____

______________________ ______________________________________

____

______________________ ______________________________________

____

Cornelius Langston Henderson

Cornelius L. Henderson has left his mark on this earth. As an engineer he has designed and built famous factories, tunnels, and bridges throughout the United States, Canada, Jamaica, Trinidad, New Zealand, Australia, and many countries in South America.

Cornelius was born in Detroit, but when his father became president of Morris Brown College, a primarily black college in Atlanta, Georgia, his family moved there. So Cornelius received his early education in the South. His outstanding achievements in mathematics and mechanics were noted, and when he graduated from high school he studied first at Morris Brown, then at Wayne University, graduating in 1906. He continued his education and received his civil engineering degree from the University of Michigan.

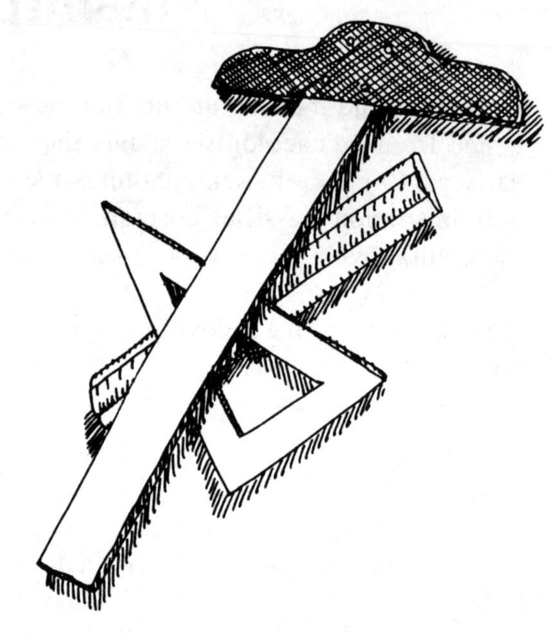

Cornelius Langston Henderson
(1887-?)
Engineer and Builder

Cornelius contributed to the design and construction of the Quebec and Thousand Island Bridge over the St. Lawrence River, the Ambassador Bridge at Detroit, the vertical lift bridges across Welland Canal, and other highways, roads, and bridges throughout Canada. Cornelius is also known for the design and construction of factory buildings in Canada and the United States. The Ford Motor Company building of Canada, the General Motors Corporation building, the Chrysler Corporation building, and many others are all to his credit. The Supreme Court building in Ottawa, Canada, the Royal Air Force hangar at Trenton, and the Royal Canadian Mounted Police building are all Canadian government buildings designed by Cornelius.

Cornelius Henderson had become a famous engineer, but he became even more famous when he constructed the General Electric Company factory building at Peterborough. As Canada's designing engineer, Cornelius traveled throughout the world designing and constructing projects.

Natural Architect

It has been said that Cornelius Henderson was a natural architect because he could design gracious buildings seemingly without much effort. Spiders are said to be natural architects too.

Most spiders show their architectural abilities in the webs that they spin. Although all spiders do not spin webs, those that do spin them do not do so for architectural beauty. The webs are used to trap insects for food.

The orb weaver spiders spin the most beautiful and complicated webs of all. Design a beautiful web for this orb weaver spider.

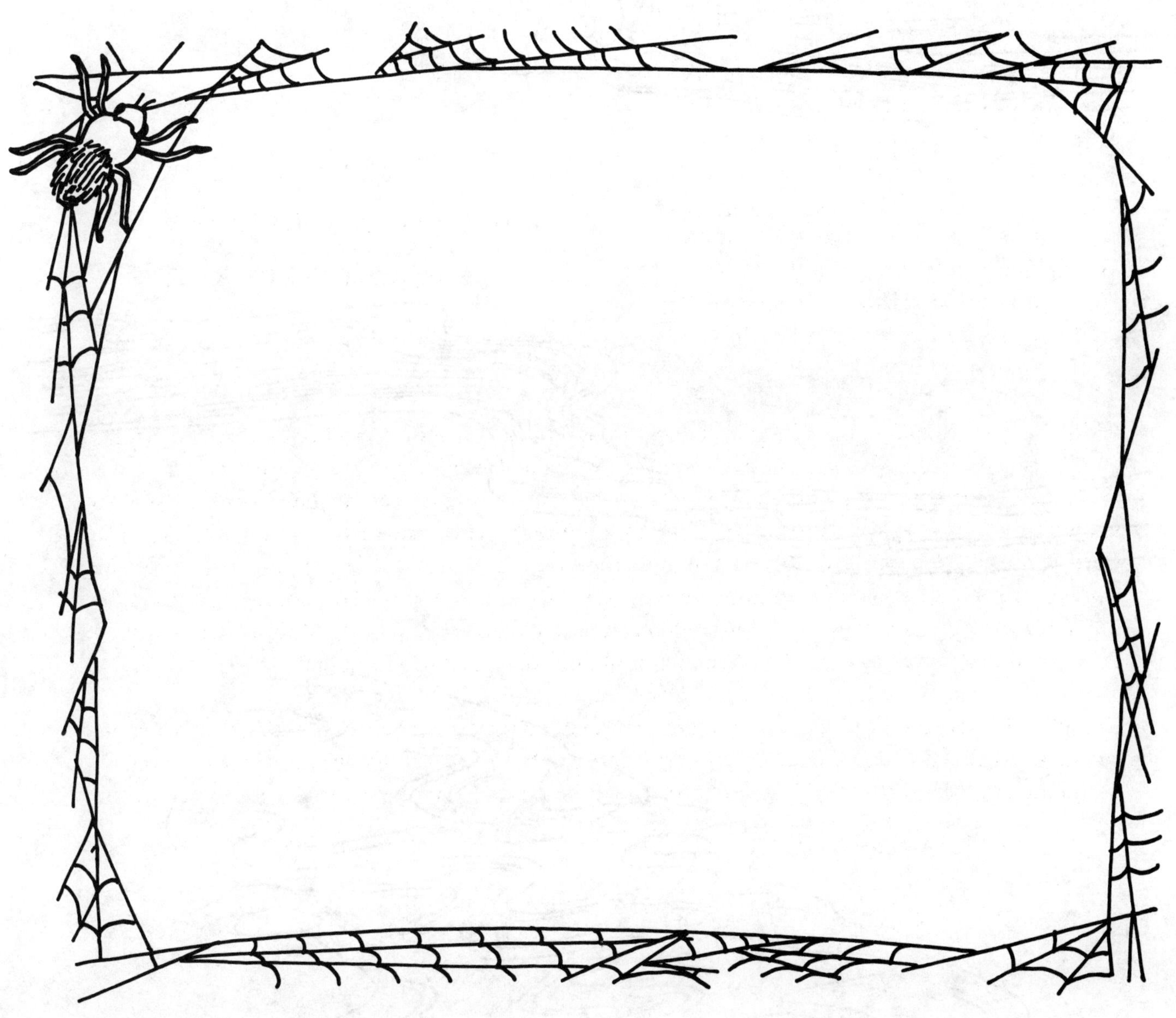

Bridge Designer

Cornelius Henderson was a designer and builder of bridges and other structures. Show your bridge-designing abilities. Draw a different bridge across each body of water below.

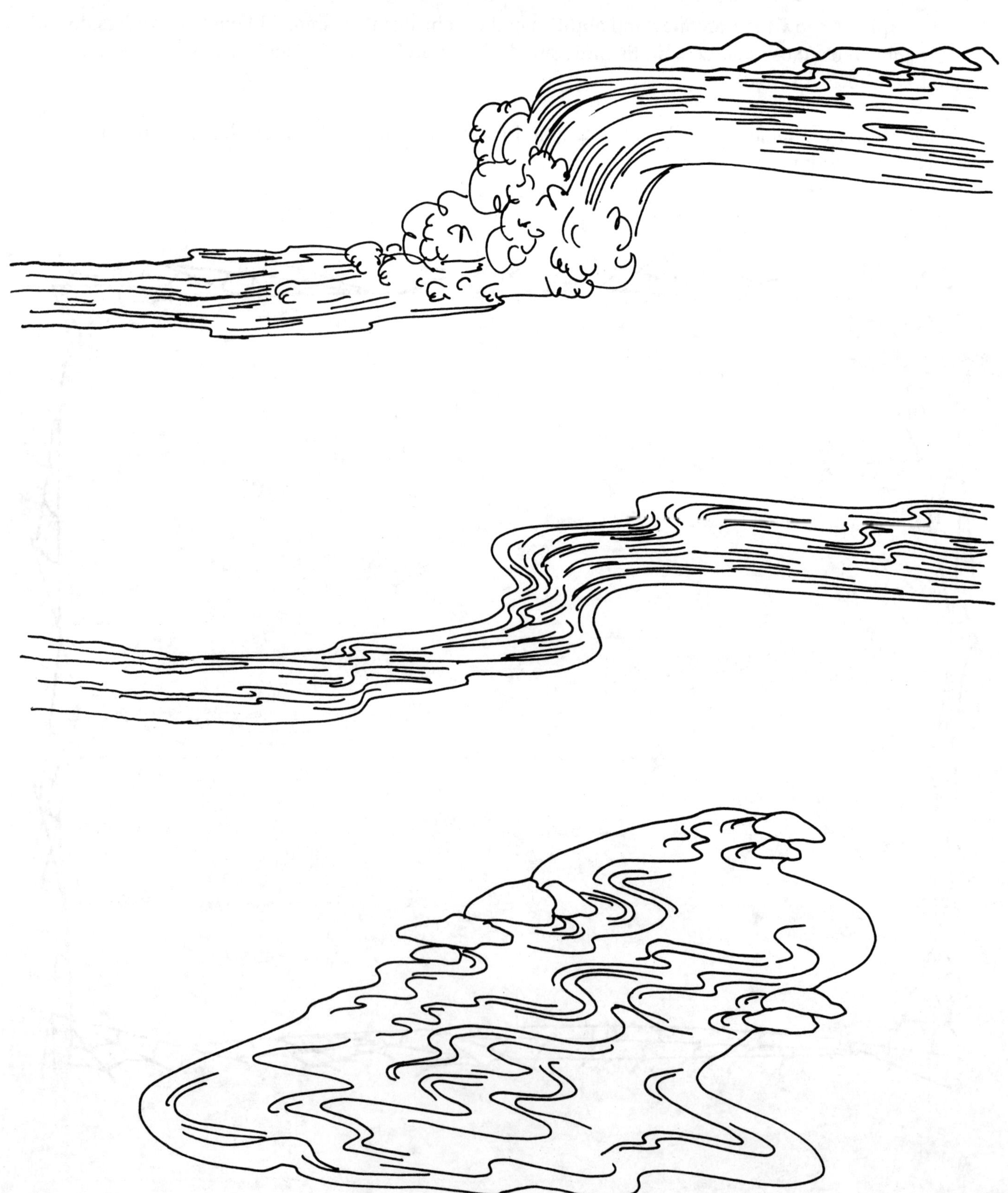

Seven Wonders

Cornelius Henderson designed and built many famous buildings and structures. Using information from his biography, list seven of these structures.

1. ____________ 2. ____________ 3. ____________

4. ____________ 5. ____________ 6. ____________

7. ____________

In ancient times the Greeks and Romans compiled a list of memorable things that travelers should see. They called their list the Seven Wonders of the Ancient World.

Since that time, writers, explorers and world travelers have compiled a list of the Seven Natural Wonders and the Seven Wonders of the Modern World.

Research and list the Seven Wonders of the Modern World.

1. ____________ 2. ____________ 3. ____________

4. ____________ 5. ____________ 6. ____________

7. ____________

Select one of the Modern Wonders and write an informational paragraph about it.

____

____

____

____

Design the eighth wonder of the modern world and write a paragraph telling all about it. Tell what it is, where it is located, why it should be the eighth wonder of the world, and any other information that you think should be included.

Designed by You

Some engineers and architects specialize in designing certain kinds of structures. Cornelius Henderson specialized in several areas. Bridges, buildings, tunnels, and factories were all his specialties.

You are an architect/engineer who specializes in designing decorations and drawings for teenagers' bedroom walls and ceilings.

In the boxes below, show some of your sample wall and ceiling decorations.

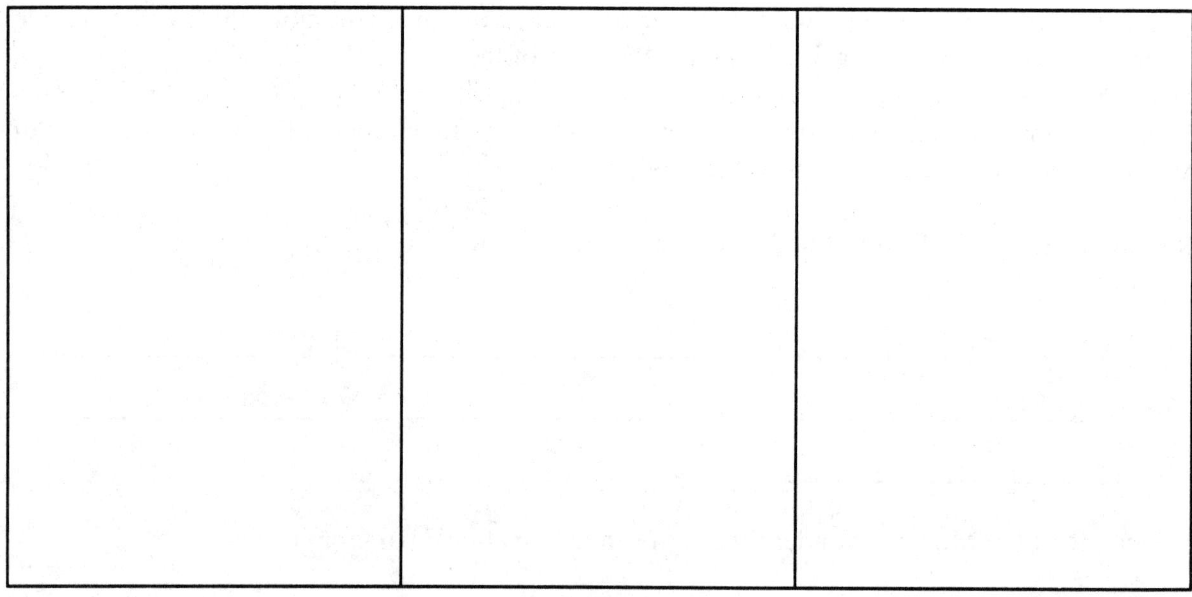

Ceiling Designs

Wall Designs

James Forten, Sr.

James Forten, Sr.
(1766-1842)
Inventor and Abolitionist

James Forten, Sr., was born free in Philadelphia in 1766. His parents were born free but his grandparents had been brought to America as slaves. His parents, Thomas and Sarah Forten, believed that their son should get a good education. They believed that his success would depend on it. They sent their son to the free school of Anthony Benzet, a renowned Quaker abolitionist, for his early education. When James was eight years old he began working beside his father in a sail loft–a factory for making sails for ships.

When he was nine years old his father died in a boating accident. So James had to end his formal education and work in a grocery store to help support his mother. When he was fourteen years old, he entered the Navy and served during the Revolutionary War. It was there that he invented a device for handling ship sails. When he returned home he worked beside Robert Bridges who owned a sail loft. When Bridges grew older, James borrowed the money from him and bought the sail loft. At the age of thirty-two James had a work force of thirty-two persons at his sail loft. As owner of the sail loft, he employed both black and white workers. James managed his loft well and became a highly respected, wealthy businessman. He made a fortune with his innovative sail making. He used much of his money to help slaves gain their freedom and to finance abolition activities.

James Forten, Sr., inventor, businessman and civil rights worker, became wealthy and used his wealth to help humanity. He built a luxurious three-story home for his wife Charlotte on Lombard Street in Philadelphia. This home later served as a station in the Underground Railroad where slaves escaped to freedom.

Problem Solver

Almost all inventors invent to solve a problem. James Forten saw a need for a device to handle ship sails so he invented one.

Choose a problem from the list below and invent a device to help solve the problem.

air pollution	poverty
crime	war
birth defects	water pollution

Draw and label the invention.

Write a television commercial to sell your invention.

Convenient Inventions

Inventions and discoveries have changed the way we live as we dream and create things that make our lives better. Think of an invention for each of the categories and tell how it has changed our lives.

Category	Invention	How It Has Changed Our Lives
1. Education	computer	Makes classwork faster and easier
2. Recreation		
3. Transportation		
4. Medicine		
5. Food		

Select one of the categories and tell how it will have changed by the year 3000.

Sweet Invention

All inventions are not technical in nature. Anything that you create, design, or dream up is an invention. Candy is one of the world's most popular snacks. There are more than 2000 different kinds of candy. The United States produces more candy than any other country.

You have just been hired by the Too Good Candy Company of New York. Your first assignment is to create a new candy bar, one that will taste better and outsell all other candy bars.

Research the different types of candy to help you create this new and different candy bar.

Name your candy bar and design a wrapper for it.

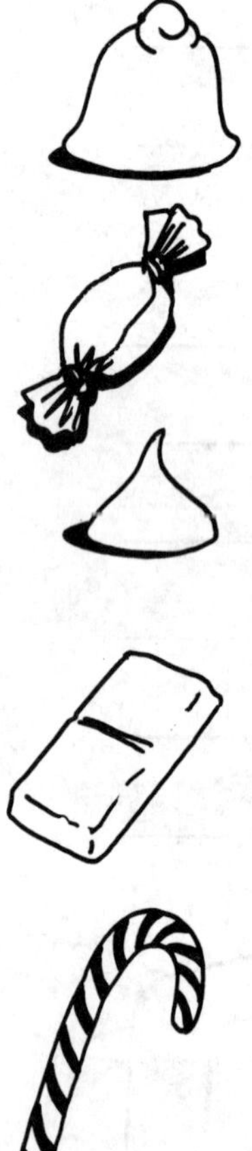

Write a television commercial to advertise your new candy bar.

____

____

____

____

Invention-of-the-Month

You are a member of the Invention-of-the-Month Club in which each member has to write a report on one inventor for each month. For each of the calendar pages below, name an inventor and write a paragraph of information about each.

January

Inventor's Name: ____________________

Information: ____________________

____

____

____

____

February

Inventor's Name: ____________________

Information: ____________________

____

____

____

____

March

Inventor's Name: ____________________

Information: ____________________

____

____

____

____

April

Inventor's Name: ____________________

Information: ____________________

____

____

____

____

May

Inventor's Name: ____________________

Information: ____________________

____

____

____

____

Albert J. Cassell

When Albert Cassell was growing up in Baltimore, Maryland, he liked to sketch and draw. It wasn't long before he had completed his early education and finished high school. He took his interest in drawing and sketching to the School of Architecture at Cornell University. No sooner had he begun his studies when World War I began and he left to serve in the Army. After the war, he and architect W.A. Hazel designed five buildings on the campus of Tuskegee University, a primarily black, prestigious college in Alabama.

Albert J. Cassell
(1895-1969)
Architect and Draftsman

In 1921 Cassell began a career in architecture at Howard University in Washington, D.C. He drafted and designed the school gymnasium and an athletic field in 1924. In 1926 he designed buildings for the University's School of Medicine. In 1931 and 1933 he designed three women's dormitories and the chemistry building. His most outstanding project on the Howard University campus was the Founders Library, designed in 1946. His largest architecture project of all was a five-million-dollar apartment complex, the Mayfair Mansions, in Washington, D.C. His architecture can be seen in other prominent places in this country as well as in Africa.

Sketch Pad

When Albert Cassell was growing up, he liked to sketch and draw. Sketch or draw your version of each thing below. Color your picture with crayons or markers.

Home Sweet Home

Most architects are general practitioners who design many different kinds of buildings. Some architects are specialists who design houses, schools or other buildings. Albert Cassell specialized in designing educational buildings and apartments.

You are an architect specialist. You design homes for animals. Design and sketch a home for each animal below. After you've designed a home for each animal, draw a floor plan of one of the homes, and design furniture that would be suitable for this animal.

Willy the Woodpecker

Annie the Ant

Robbie the Rabbit

Cassie the Cat

Alphabet Houses

Some architects design buildings that are shaped like the letter *A*. This is called the A-frame style. Build a house design around these letters.

M

V

B

S

C

T

Now and Then I

Pick three objects from the crystal ball. Cut out pictures of these objects from magazines and paste them under the *Now* column.

Complete the chart by drawing what you think the object will look like 100 years from now.

Now	In 100 Years

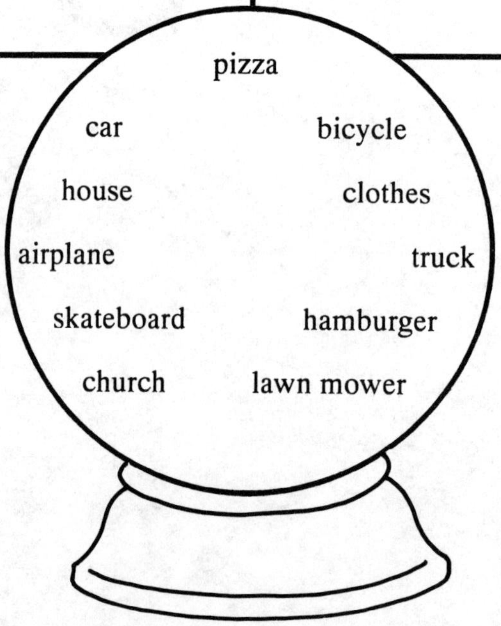

pizza
car
bicycle
house
clothes
airplane
truck
skateboard
hamburger
church
lawn mower

Ernest Everett Just

Ernest Everett Just
(1883-1941)
Distinguished Biological Scientist

Dr. Ernest Everett Just was a cytologist. A cytologist is a person who studies cells. Our bodies are made of cells. If our cells stop functioning, then we stop functioning and eventually die. Dr. Just spent most of his life studying cells. He studied the cells of marine (ocean) animals and discovered many new facts.

Ernest Everett Just was born in Charleston, South Carolina, on August 14, 1883. His father was a dock worker and his mother was a school teacher. When Ernest was four years old, his father died, and Ernest was forced to work in the fields to earn money to help his mother with the family income. When he completed high school, his mother sent him north to better schools. Ernest enrolled in Kimball Union Academy and graduated at the top of his class. He faced many instances of injustice and prejudice, but this did not stop him. He entered Dartmouth College and graduated with degrees in history and biology. In 1916 he received a Ph.D. degree with honors from the University of Chicago.

For twenty years Dr. Just examined and studied cells. He felt that the more we knew about cells and their functions, the quicker we would be able to combat diseases such as cancer, leukemia, sickle cell anemia, and other cellular diseases.

For his accomplishments, Dr. Just received numerous honors and awards. In 1915 he became the first person to receive the Spingarn Medal. The Spingarn Medal is awarded to an African American person who has made outstanding achievement in his or her chosen field, and certainly Dr. Just deserved such an award.

With all of his accomplishments in science, Dr. Just was never invited to conduct research in an American laboratory, but he was invited to both Germany and Paris, France. In Germany he conducted research at the Kaiser Wilhelm Institute of Biology, the world's greatest academy of physics, chemistry, and biology.

In 1941 Dr. Just died of cancer. He was a dedicated scientist, and we are all better off for the discoveries that he made.

Cytologist

Dr. Ernest Just was a cytologist. A cytologist uses a microscope to study cells–the tiny units that make up all living things.

Label the parts of this microscope.

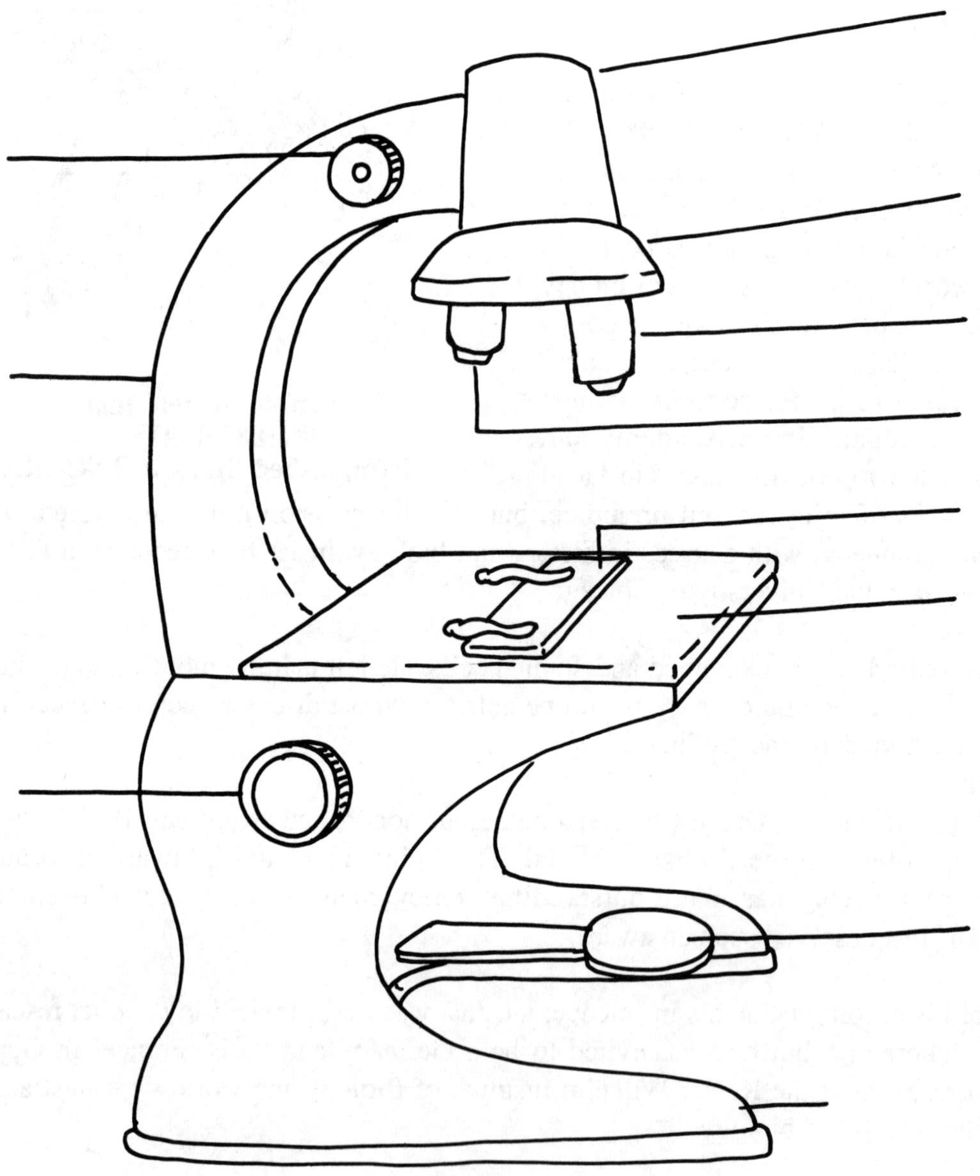

Use reference materials to learn more about microscopes. On the back of this sheet, write an information paragraph about the microscope.

The Spingarn

In 1915 Dr. Ernest Just became the first person to be awarded the Spingarn Medal.

Write an information paragraph on the Spingarn Medal.

Write an information paragraph on Joel Spingarn.

Sketch a picture of the front and back of the Spingarn Medal on the back of this page.

Cell It!

The human body is made up of billions of cells. Each type of cell has its own shape and its own function or job. At this very moment cells in your body are performing their different jobs. As you read these words, nerve cells in your eye are carrying messages to your brain. Muscle cells are helping to move your eyeball from one word to another. Skin cells are protecting your body by keeping out diseases, and blood cells are helping to fight germs and bacteria that enter the body.

Make a sketch of these types of cells.

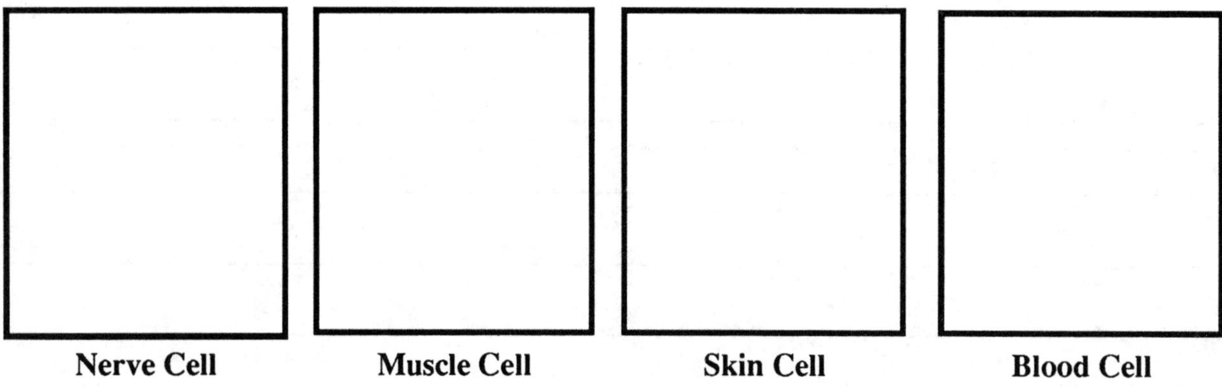

In the body, like cells group together to form tissue, and tissues are grouped together to form an organ. Listed below are five organs of the human body. Tell what each organ does.

Liver: ____

Brain: ____

Spleen: ____

Stomach: ____

Heart: ____

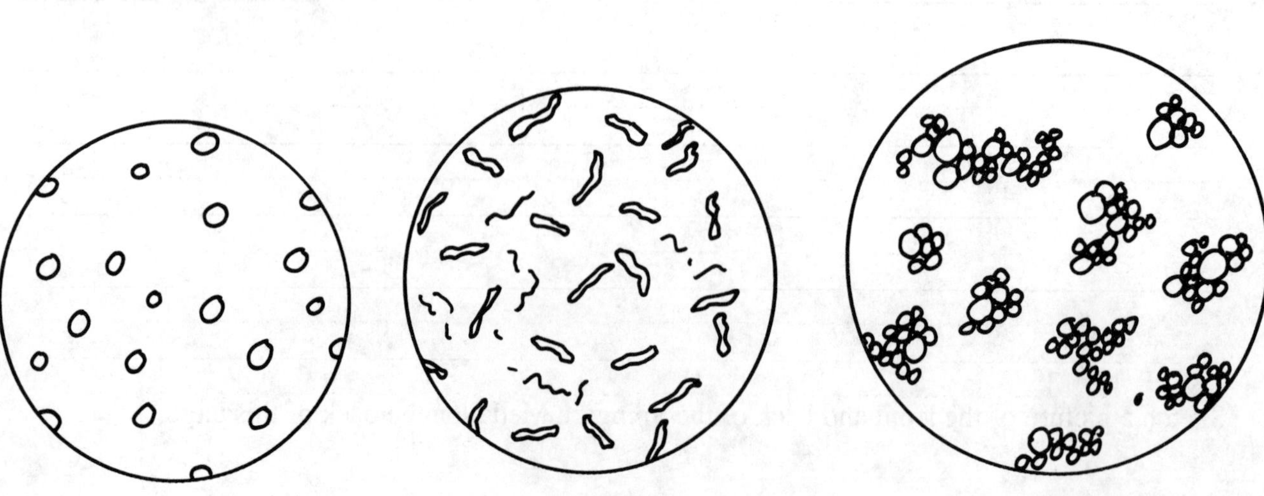

Peace

As an African American, Dr. Just faced many instances of injustice and prejudice. This means that he was not treated fairly.

Imagine that you have been organizing a Peace Club at your school to help people of all groups get along with one another.

Fill in the information about your club.

What is the name of your club? ______________________________

What is its symbol? ______________________________

Design a uniform for the club.

List things that your club will do to promote peace.

____

____

____

____

____

On another piece of paper, design a mini poster asking students to join the club.

Percy Lavon Julian

Percy Lavon Julian
(1899-1975)
Research Chemist, Millionaire, and Teacher

What do kings, cabbages and you have in common? If you were to ask Percy Julian, he would tell you that kings, cabbages, and you are all made of chemical substances called elements and compounds. Dr. Julian knew a lot about chemical elements and compounds because he was a chemist.

In order to become a chemist, Dr. Julian began just as you and I began. He went to elementary school, then to high school. His mother was a teacher who knew the value of a good education. When Percy was growing up in Montgomery, Alabama, she sent him to a private school. When he graduated from high school, he attended college at DePauw University in Indiana. When he graduated from DePauw, he wanted to continue his education, but because he was African American, the leading graduate schools would not accept him. So he took a job teaching chemistry at Fisk University, a prestigious black college in Nashville, Tennessee. Two years later he went to Harvard University and continued his study in chemistry. He received a master's degree in chemistry and taught at West Virginia State College and Howard University in Washington, D.C.

In 1929 Julian studied abroad, at Vienna, Austria, and earned his Ph.D. degree in chemistry and became interested in soybean research.

After returning to the United States, he created a drug called physostigmine, which is used to treat an eye disease called glaucoma. For this important discovery, Dr. Julian was asked to head the chemistry department at his alma mater, DePauw University. He did not get the job because he was African American. Dr. Julian became disappointed and left the university to work as a chemist with the Glidden Paint Company. In just one year Glidden Paint became one of the most prosperous paint companies in the world.

During World War II the lives of thousands of servicemen were saved with Dr. Julian's invention, "Aero-foam," a soybean product used to extinguish fires. But Dr. Julian is best known for his greatest discovery–a new way to produce cortisone in large quantities at a reasonable cost. Before his invention, this promising drug was being used to treat arthritis, but it was extremely expensive.

In 1950 Dr. Julian formed his own pharmaceutical (drug) company–Julian Laboratories in Oak Park, Illinois, and one in Mexico City. Within a few years his pharmaceutical company became one of the largest producers of drugs in the country. He later sold his Oak Park company but remained its president.

Dr. Julian died of liver cancer in 1975, but he will always be remembered for his contributions to the field of medicine and drugs to help relieve pain and suffering.

Symbolize It!

Many of the chemicals that Dr. Julian worked with had short names or symbols. Twenty of these chemical elements are written below. Write the symbol name for each element in the blank.

1. Hydrogen ______________________
2. Oxygen ______________________
3. Helium ______________________
4. Fluorine ______________________
5. Nickel ______________________
6. Nitrogen ______________________
7. Zinc ______________________
8. Silver ______________________
9. Gold ______________________
10. Copper ______________________
11. Aluminum ______________________
12. Potassium ______________________
13. Iron ______________________
14. Sodium ______________________
15. Calcium ______________________
16. Carbon ______________________
17. Mercury ______________________
18. Magnesium ______________________
19. Silicon ______________________
20. Iodine ______________________

Fill in each blank below with the correct element name.

1. Most soft drink cans are made of this. ______________________
2. It has the same name as the U.S. five-cent piece. ______________________
3. We get this element by drinking milk. ______________________
4. This element makes balloons float. ______________________
5. We need this element to breathe. ______________________

Can It!

Chemicals make up many of the fruits and vegetables that we eat. Oranges, lemons, limes, and grapefruit contain a chemical compound called citric acid. The citric acid gives these fruits a sour taste. By adding just the right amounts of citric acid to soft drinks, manufacturers are able to produce soft drinks that have a pleasantly sour flavor. Read the labels on the cans of three of your favorite soft drinks. Write the chemical ingredients on the cans below. Write the name of the soda pop beneath each can.

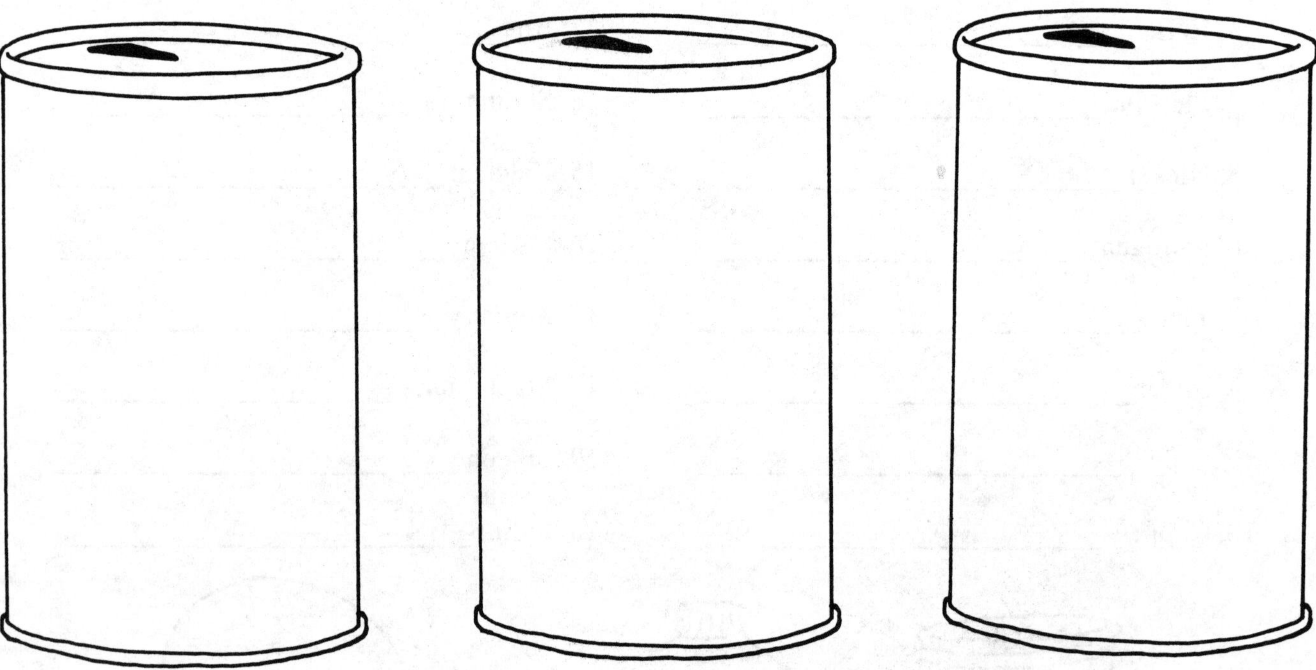

Create a new soft drink. Give it a name and design the can below for your new soft drink.

National Organizations

Dr. Julian was honored with numerous awards and citations for his medical and scientific achievements in chemistry. He was also a member of many scientific organizations.

The American Chemical Society is a nonprofit organization. Over 142,000 individual chemists and chemical engineers belong to this organization. The society began in 1937. It is designed to provide information to its members, the public, and the government. National Chemistry Week is observed the first full week of November. Its purpose is to encourage children to recognize and appreciate the many contributions of chemistry in their lives.

Do you belong to any national organizations such as the Boy Scouts or Girl Scouts?

Create an imaginary national science organization. Give your organization a name and design a badge for it, and write two paragraphs of information about it. Who can belong to the club? What are the organization's goals? What awards or special events do you sponsor? What famous people are members? Tell as much about your organization as you can. Use the back of this page if you need more space.

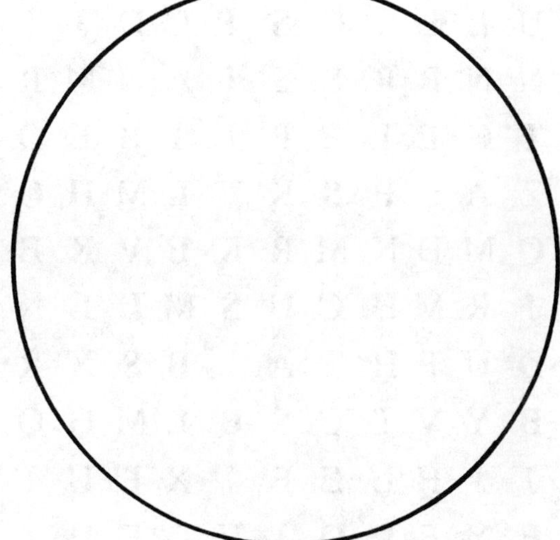

Chemical Search

Twenty chemical elements are hidden in the puzzle below. Can you find them? Look up, down, backwards, and diagonally. When you have found them all, select five from the list and write two or three important sentences about them. Use a dictionary or encyclopedia or other reference book if you need help.

Chemical Search

L P S S Q H W M H E E T Y C X U Y X R N C
C P K P Z M M K W T N U V F A M N T C A Q
E S X T S H V U W Z D I X M D T N F R S O
W N C C M F M R I S Q N D T P O E B H Z J
C U R O S U U W E C G R K O C W O O W Y T
R G H P P M I Q P I L O T I I N J Z R A G
S J W M R P S D N X U A L U M I N U M N L
N G G B L U E E O Q S I C D J T C X K T C
N V F N U N N R R S S I A N M R K K U F W
K E R H U I G E I F P I J B E O X C W Z Y
B N G R R Z A U P S K V L M H G Q K M R B
Z N Q O R Q M D N M R R E V K E Y U F D Z
B K U L R J R M H C U S M L E N F X Y E E
S L N A V D U F H T A I B S X R W T O S X
F Z E R S B Y V J C S B L M Q Q A P L S C
P Q U K R J J H L E E J X E U I B D C Z L
M Z A T C E Y E L O J V D E H I F X O Y R
S M I I I I P G B L R Q W X T B E Y P I D
L P U V U C N I Z N L Q S I U F Z O A U M

Can you find these words?

magnesium
nitrogen
silicon
iodine
copper
helium
gold

potassium
fluorine
mercury
carbon
silver
oxygen
zinc

aluminum
hydrogen
calcium
sodium
nickel
iron

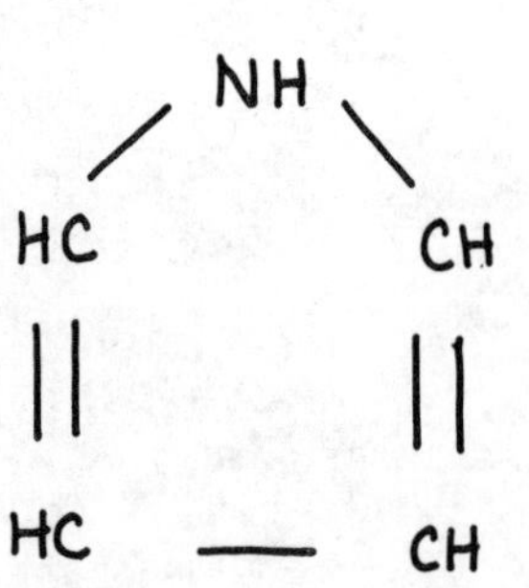

Lloyd A. Hall

Lloyd A. Hall
(1894-1971)
Food Chemist

For many of us there is nothing more satisfying than enjoying a meal of tasty food. For this great privilege we can thank, in part, Dr. Lloyd A. Hall. Dr. Hall's work as a food chemist was to make food more enjoyable and nutritious over a long period of time. He used chemicals to keep food from spoiling and to help it retain its vitamins, color, and flavor.

Dr. Hall himself had an interesting beginning. One of his grandmothers was born a slave in Alabama. She escaped on the Underground Railroad to Illinois. One of his grandfathers went to Chicago in 1837 and started the first and oldest church in Chicago. Both of Dr. Hall's parents had a high school education. This was a major accomplishment in those days. In elementary school Dr. Hall loved science. In high school he became interested in chemistry. He also liked debating and athletics. He was good in both of these activities, and he made good grades in all of his classes. After he graduated from high school he got a job and worked his way through college at Northwestern University in Illinois. He did additional studying at the University of Chicago. When Dr. Hall completed his studies, he applied for a job with Western Electric Company. He was hired by phone. When he reported for work in person, he was told that they didn't hire black people. Dr. Hall was very disappointed and disgusted, but this rejection did not stop him. He got a job as a chemist in the Chicago Department of Health Laboratories. Later his interest took a turn toward food chemistry. He became interested in the preservation and storage of food. He accepted a food processing job at the Griffith Laboratory and became chief chemist and director of research. It was here that he did his experimentations with preserving foods. While there he found several ways to keep food from spoiling. Before his work and research, common table salt was the only chemical compound that was used to preserve meat. In 1951 Dr. Hall and a friend invented a way to cure bacon that took only a few hours instead of the six to fifteen days by the old method.

Dr. Hall went on to do many more experiments on food. In all, Dr. Hall was granted 105 patents for his discoveries and inventions related to food.

Dr. Hall had received many honors, awards, and recognitions for his work in food chemistry. He was a member of many important organizations.

Dr. Hall died in 1971, but he will always be remembered for his contributions to the meat-packing industry. Without his various discoveries and recipes for curing and preserving food, we would not have the many different varieties of cured foods that we have today. So, the next time you take a bite of your breakfast bacon, think about Lloyd A. Hall.

Get Your Vitamins

Vitamins are important substances that the body needs for growth and health. Dr. Hall used chemicals to keep food from spoiling and to help it keep its color, taste, and vitamins.

Complete the Vitamin Chart to help you learn more about vitamins. One is done for you.

Vitamin Chart

Name of Vitamin	Food in Which the Vitamin Is Found	What the Vitamin Does for the Body
A	sweet potatoes, milk, liver, eggs, butter, green and yellow vegetables	Needed for healthy skin, eyes, respiratory and digestive systems, normal growth of bones and teeth, and to help you see better at night.

New Vitamin

The time is in the future. You have discovered a new vitamin. Design the bottle label for your new vitamin.

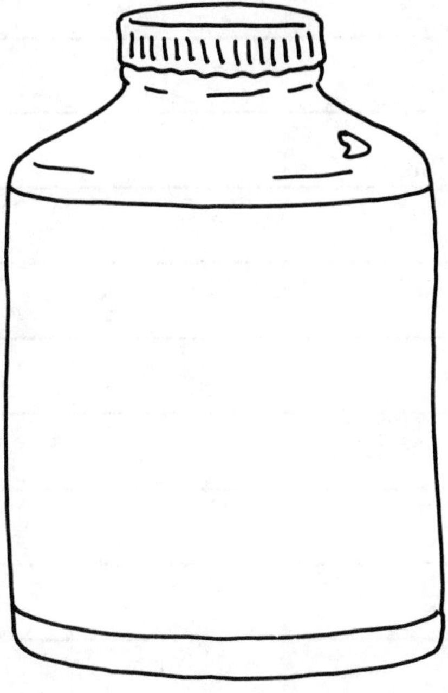

Write a television commercial to advertise your new vitamin telling all of the things that it can do for the body.

Food for Thought

Listed below are several words related to food. Use a dictionary or encyclopedia to help you write a definition for each "food" word.

1. food additive: ____________________

____

2. Food and Drug Administration: ____________________

____

3. food chain: ____________________

____

4. food coloring: ____________________

____

5. food poisoning: ____________________

____

6. food preservation: ____________________

____

7. Food and Agriculture Organization: ____________________

____

8. food supply: ____________________

____

9. Food Stamp Program: ____________________

____

10. food spoilage: ____________________

____

Food Groups

Scientists divide the food that we eat into four basic groups shown on the wheel below. Dr. Lloyd Hall worked mostly with foods in the meat group.

Research the different food groups and the number of servings you should have from each group every day. On the wheel list foods for each, and write the number of servings needed each day. On the back of this page, tell why it is important to eat a balanced diet.

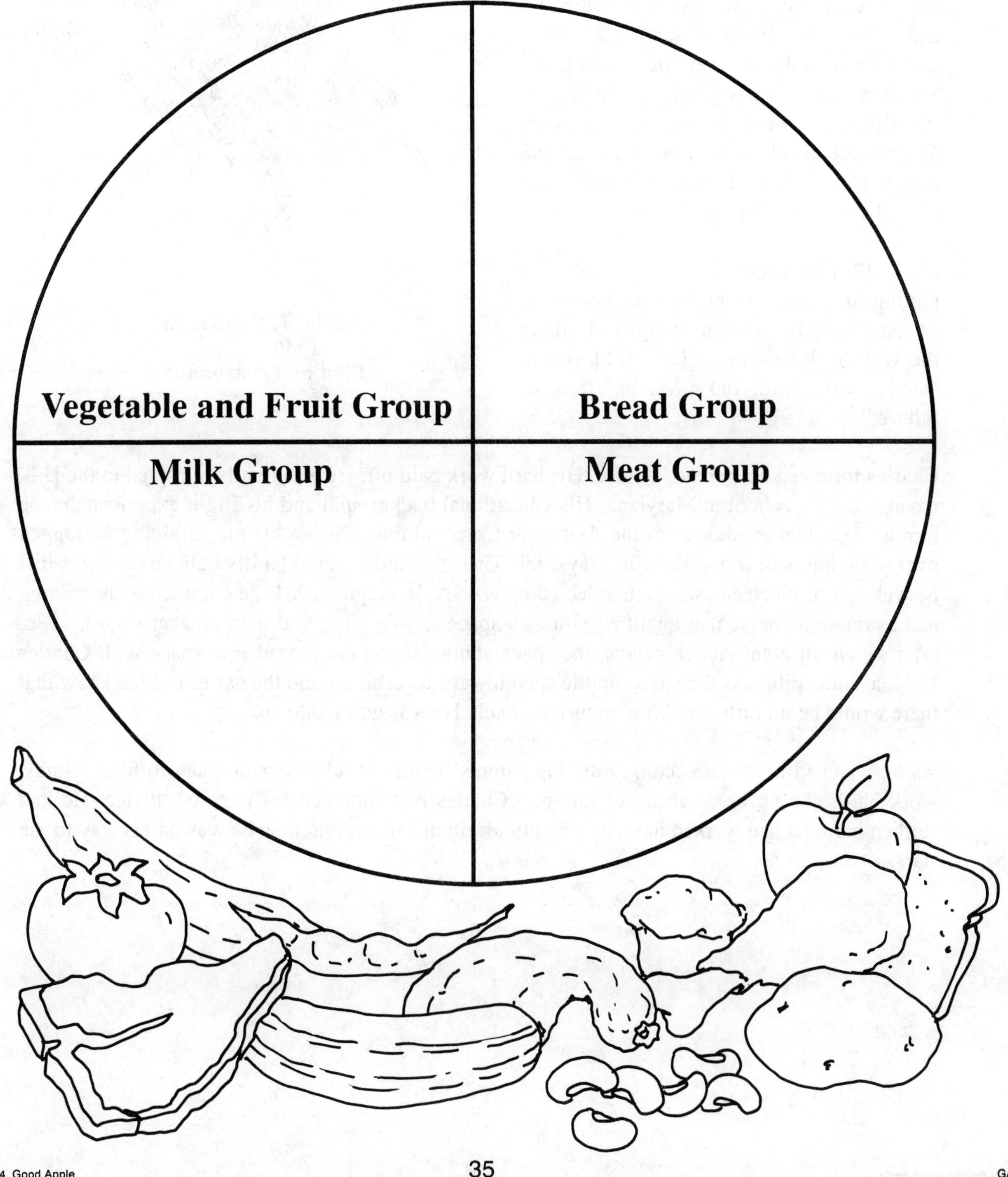

Charles F. Bolden, Jr.

When Charles Bolden was growing up in his hometown of Columbia, South Carolina, he dreamed of becoming an astronaut. He spent hours reading science fiction books and dreaming of himself aboard a space shuttle headed into space. When he finished high school in 1964, he enrolled in the U.S. Naval Academy at Annapolis. He earned a B.S. degree in electrical science in 1968; then he joined the Marines and served in the Vietnam War as a naval aviator. He applied for test pilot school but was turned down. To improve his chances of getting accepted, he continued his education at USC and earned a master's degree.

Charles F. Bolden, Jr.
(1946-)
Pilot and Astronaut

He knew that each educational step was putting him closer to his goal of becoming an astronaut. He was encouraged all along the way by his parents. They told him to "study, work hard, and never be afraid of failure."

Charles followed his parents' advice. His hard work paid off. He was finally accepted in the U.S. naval test pilot school in Maryland. His educational background and his flight experience made him an excellent candidate for the Astronaut Corp training. During his pilot training he logged over 4000 hours of flying time. In May 1980, Charles Bolden could hardly believe the news that he was one of nineteen astronauts selected by NASA. In August 1981, he completed his training and evaluation course that qualified him as a space shuttle pilot, and then on January 12, 1986, after seven different launch delays, the space shuttle *Columbia* roared into space with Charles Bolden as the pilot. As the space shuttle sped toward its orbit around the earth, Bolden knew that there would be no further delays, no turning back. He was going into space.

As he watched his dreams come true, his parents' words of advice came back to him. "Study, work hard, and never be afraid of failure." Charles had followed his parents' advice. He had studied hard, he had worked hard, he was not afraid of failure, and now he was on his way to the stars.

Lift-Off!

You are an astronaut trainee for a future space mission, but before you take off you must complete the ten activities in the space rocket. When you complete an activity, color in the corresponding rocket section. Begin with 1 and work toward 10.

Advice, Advice, Advice

Advice, advice, advice. Your parents, relatives, teachers, and friends are always giving you advice. Charles Bolden's parents gave him this advice: "Study, work hard, and never be afraid of failure." He followed their advice and became a successful astronaut. What advice have your parents, relatives, teachers, or friends given you?

Parents: ____________________

Relatives: ____________________

Teachers: ____________________

Friends: ____________________

NEVER BE AFRAID OF FAILURE! (GRANDAD)
READ! (Dad)
PRACTICE! (Aunt)
ASK QUESTIONS! (Uncle)
ADVICE ENTRY #101
STUDY! (Dad)
WORK HARD! (Mom)

If you could give some advice to your parents, relatives, teachers and friends, what would you say?

Parents: ____________________

Relatives: ____________________

Teachers: ____________________

Friends: ____________________

Space-Age Math

If you are interested in becoming an astronaut, engineer or space scientist, math is one of the subjects that you will have to study. At the U.S. Naval Academy at Annapolis, Charles Bolden studied many forms of math. Practice your math by solving these problems. Gravity is the force that attracts and holds objects on the surface of the earth. The force of gravity is different on the other planets. If you know your weight on earth, then you can calculate your weight on other planets by multiplying your weight by the gravity factor of each planet. You can multiply using decimals or fractions. Round your answers off to the nearest whole number.

Planet	Your Weight on Earth	Gravity Factor	Your Weight on That Planet
Mercury		0.38 or $^{3}/_{8}$	
Venus		0.91 or $^{9}/_{10}$	
Mars		0.38 or $^{3}/_{8}$	
Jupiter		2.5 or 2 $^{1}/_{2}$	
Saturn		1.07 or 1 $^{1}/_{14}$	
Uranus		0.93 or $^{14}/_{15}$	
Neptune		1.2 or 1 $^{1}/_{5}$	
Pluto		0.03 or $^{1}/_{33}$	

Space Maze

Help Herbie the Astronaut find his lost spaceship.

Lewis Howard Latimer

Lewis Howard Latimer
(1848-1928)
Pioneer Electrician and Draftsman

The telephone–what in the world would we do without it? How would we summon help, make appointments, and call friends?

Lewis Latimer did not invent the telephone, but he drew the blueprints for it. In 1876, when Alexander Graham Bell needed a highly skilled draftsman to make drawings of his new invention, the telephone, Lewis Latimer was given the job.

These drawings were just one of the many important things that Lewis Latimer did during his lifetime. He was also a pioneer in the development of the electric light bulb. He was the only African American member of the Edison Pioneers, a group of outstanding scientists and inventors who worked with Thomas Edison.

Latimer was born in Chelsea, Massachusetts, in 1848, but he grew up in the city of Boston. Latimer was skilled in mechanical drawing. This enabled him to get a job as a draftsman for a patent solicitor. While working, Lewis Latimer was fascinated by the drawings and taught himself to be really good.

In 1878 Latimer worked for Hiram Maxim, who invented the machine gun. Latimer also worked with the U.S. Electric Lighting Company. Here he worked to improve the carbon filament in light bulbs. His most important invention was the improvement of the light bulb filament–the tiny wires inside the light bulb. In 1882 he received a patent for his new light bulb. In 1884 Latimer worked for the Edison Company where he supervised the installation of Edison's lighting systems in New York, Philadelphia, Canada, and London.

Latimer was not interested in science only. He was a man of many talents and skills. He wrote and published a volume of love poems. He was also the author of a book entitled *Incandescent Lighting*. He worked as a civil rights leader and taught mechanical drawing and English. When he died in 1928, his death was mourned around the world.

On May 10, 1968, a school in New York honored this great electrical genius by giving his name to its building. The Lewis H. Latimer Public School in Brooklyn, New York, stands as a monument to this great African American scientist.

A Meeting of Great Minds

One day Lewis Latimer met Alexander Graham Bell. A friendship developed, and Bell asked Latimer to make the drawings for his newest invention–the telephone.

You are a gifted designer. What have the following famous persons asked you to design?

1. Bryant Gumbel–journalist ____________________

2. The President of the United States: ____________________

3. Bill Cosby–comedian and actor: ____________________

4. Michael Jordan–famous basketball player: ____________________

5. Jesse Jackson–civil rights leader: ____________________

6. Gwendolyn Brooks–writer of poetry: ____________________

7. Oprah Winfrey–talk show hostess: ____________________

8. Colin Powell–chairman of the Joint Chiefs of Staff (military): ____________________

9. Malcolm-Jamal Warner–actor: ____________________

10. Mae Jemison–astronaut: ____________________

Now and Then II

Many inventions that started out as original designs have now been changed over the years.

Listed below are five of these inventions. Make sketches in the appropriate boxes to show how each invention looked originally, how it looks today, and how you think it will look in the future.

Invention	Then	Now	Future
1. Television			
2. Chair			
3. Car			
4. Bed			
5. Cooking stove			

The Ladder of Invention

Listed below are ten inventions. Place them in chronological order on the invention ladder. Research two of the inventions and write a paragraph of information about each on another sheet of paper.

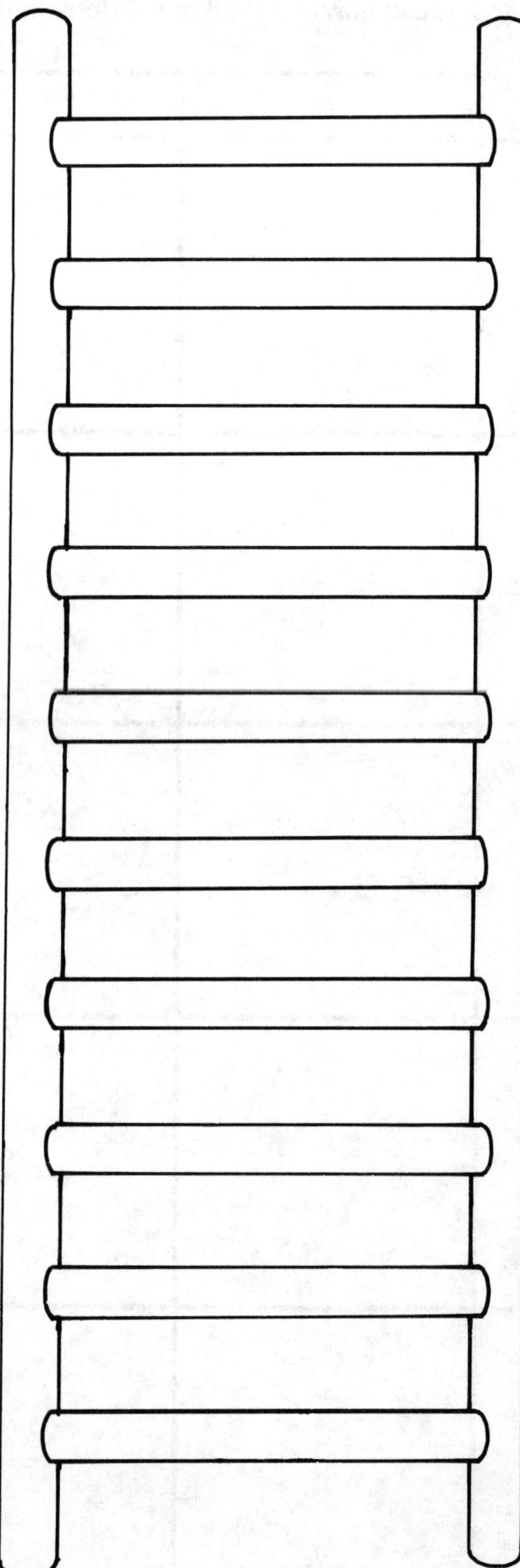

Stethoscope–	1816
Dynamite–	1867
Zipper–	1893
Airplane–	1903
Compound Microscope–	1590
Laser–	1960
Radar–	1935
Telescope–	1608
Thermometer–	1593
Steam Engine–	1698

Dr. Seek and You

Dr. Seek and you have been working in the laboratory for months on an invention that would make great changes in the lives of all people in the world. Your invention is finally finished, and you have been asked to announce the invention to the world. You are scheduled to appear on Channel WSEEK TV's Mid-Morning Show. The world is waiting to hear what the invention is and how all people will benefit from it. It is the night before the telecast and you are writing your speech. Write what you will say in the space below. Use the back of this page or another sheet of paper if you need more space.

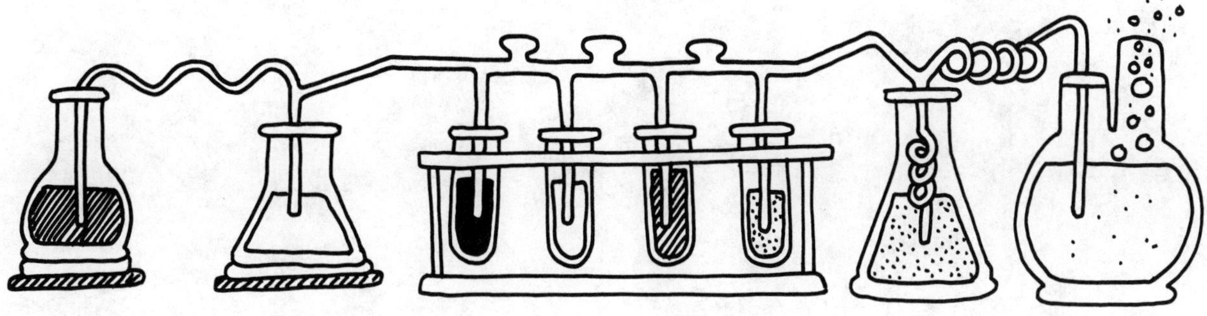

Louis Temple

Louis Temple
(1800-1854)
Inventor

People have hunted whales since prehistoric times. In earlier days whales were captured and killed for their meat and for whale oil that was used in lamps and as cooking oil. Today whale oil is used in making many different products such as makeup, soap, and varnish. At first large numbers of whales were killed by whaling fleets which endangered the survival of some kinds of whales. Now, the International Whaling Committee has placed a limit on the number of whales that may be killed each year.

Louis Temple was born a slave in Richmond, Virginia, in 1800. He later moved to New Bedford, Massachusetts, and became a successful blacksmith. Whaling was a big industry in Massachusetts. It provided thousands of jobs for the people there. While making whale-hunting tools for the whalers at his blacksmith shop, Louis Temple heard the whalers talk of the whales that often struggled free from the harpoons that they were using. (A harpoon is a spear or javelin used in whale hunting.) Louis Temple decided that he could produce a harpoon that would lock the whale onto the harpoon so that it could not get away. He invented the Temple Toggle. Other scientists and inventors called his invention "the single most important invention in the whole history of whaling." It is not known why, but Temple did not get a patent on his Temple Toggle. So other whalers quickly copied his toggle design and began producing Temple's Toggle. It is said that other companies produced over 13,000 toggles between 1848 and 1868. Although Louis Temple did prosper from the sales of his toggle, this was hardly anything compared to the money that he could have made if he had gotten a patent for his invention.

He did, however, become prosperous enough to build a larger blacksmith shop. He died before the larger new shop was completed. His death was due to an injury that he received when he stumbled over a piece of lumber used to build his shop. The lumber had been left by a careless city worker. He sued the city of New Bedford but was unable to reach a settlement before his death. As a result of this tragedy, Louis Temple died a poor man. After paying debts associated with the new blacksmith shop, his wife and son had but a little money left.

Stop It!

During Louis Temple's lifetime whaling was a major industry. Temple's hometown of New Bedford, Massachusetts, became one of the chief American whaling ports. Today, only Japan and Russia have large whaling industries. In 1962 excessive whale killing greatly reduced the world's whale population. In 1971 the United States federal government outlawed whaling and the import of whale products. In 1974 antiwhaling groups (people against whaling) campaigned to end whaling. These protestors wrote brochures and made speeches urging people not to buy products from Japan and Russia until these countries stop whaling.

Is there something that you think people should stop doing? Make a list of ten of these actions. One is listed for you.
Example:

1. Stop smoking
2. ______________________
3. ______________________
4. ______________________
5. ______________________
6. ______________________
7. ______________________
8. ______________________
9. ______________________
10. ______________________

Choose one action from the list and write a speech telling why people should stop the action. Research information to be used in your speech. Use the back of this page if you need more space. Use the information in your speech to make a brochure asking people to stop the action.

The One That Got Away

Louis Temple was not a whale hunter. He was a blacksmith. In his blacksmith shop he made harpoons and other equipment used to catch whales. While making equipment for whale hunters, he often heard whalers talk about the whales that got away. This is what gave Temple the idea for his invention of the Temple Toggle.

Sometimes fishermen tell tall tales about "the one that got away." Write a tall tale beginning with this story starter: One day as Uncle Bunkie and I were resting lazily on the banks of the pond, my fishing line began to jerk; then there was a large splash. I jumped to my feet and began pulling in my line. I could not believe my eyes! There on the end of my line was . . .

Making It Better

Some inventors improve things that have already been invented. Show how you would improve the following objects by adding to the drawings below.

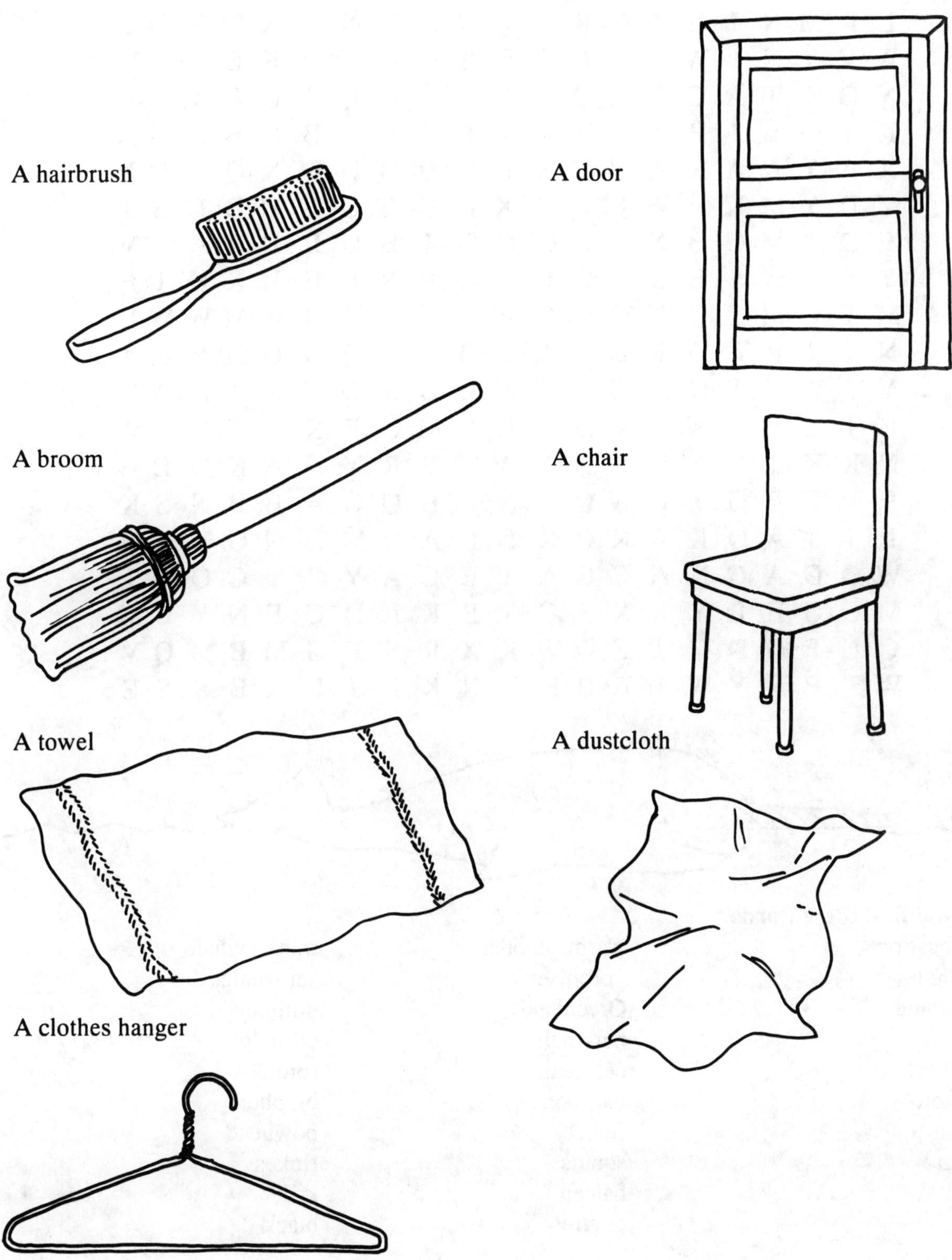

Whale Words

Thirty whaling words are hidden in the puzzle below. Can you find all of them? Be sure to look up, down, backward, and diagonally.

Whale Words

```
L R M N J H W O R W Z U D X N B N O N D J
W V Y N Y W T D L T D S A G U L E B A S W
N O I T A C O L O H C E E C Q D C E I F U
R T O L I P I L M L T L D K A B H B Q G A
X A Y A A R A N U N P O B O U W X Q S U P
Y D Y M K H W F P O X H U L O L M B L S J
F D I M C B X X U O G W I B U L F R A E V
Y P U A S E S I O P R O P N P E B X H I E
M T C M T Q N Q H R E L E Y S N W M W W L
N I J R E O P E Q A E B H T Q O U H R H A
Y J W A T N M Z E H N B U R R T K A A A H
B T C F Q W F V D L L L M O P K C C N L W
N K K J S A D R J A A U P R Y N A K D E E
R V C B G J B W C F N B B Q G A B B N S K
L I J A O K A K Q K D B A U M L N G V D N
W O D A C N A E C A T E C A Y P I C Q I I
M O G H L Y X X F C Y R K L D C F N Y U M
C U F G D C J F W W K X R S F G M B M Q V
W T P S Y W I E B H U R K F J L X B S S E
```

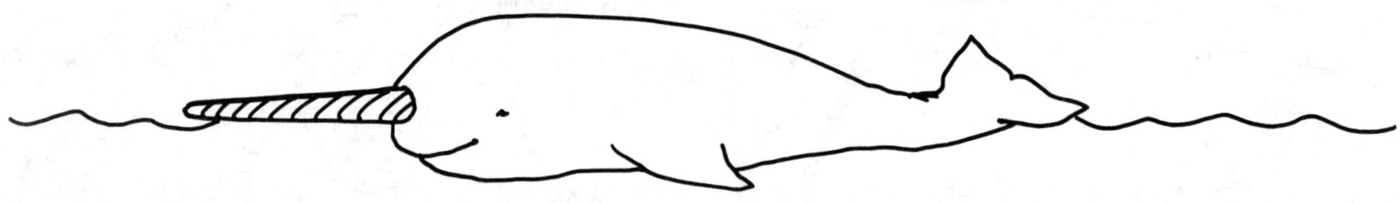

Can you find these words?

echolocation
blow holes
blue whale
buoyancy
humpback
plankton
belugas
diatom
mammal
pilot

warm-blooded
porpoises
Greenland
narwhals
cetacean
harpoon
finback
squids
baleen
pygmy

minke whale
sei whales
dolphins
cachalot
rorquals
blubber
bowhead
flukes
krill
black

Select ten words from the list and tell how each is related to whaling.

Robert Pelham, Jr.

Robert Pelham, Jr.
(1859-1943)
Inventor, Politician, Journalist, and Government Official

Do you know what a census is? A census is a way of counting the number of people who live in a country. A census also provides information about the age, employment, income, and race of a group of people. The U.S. Census Bureau in Washington, D.C., conducts a census population count every five years in years ending with zero or five, such as 1990 and 1995. The Census Bureau surveys people to get information; then it tabulates or counts the results. Finally, the results are made known to the public. Can you imagine the calculations and numbers that the Bureau has to deal with in counting every person in the United States? In 1900 Robert Pelham, Jr., was appointed a clerk in the United States Census Bureau. During his thirty-seven years of working at the Bureau, he saw a need for a machine that would count and tabulate the census information faster than a human could, so he invented a machine that would do the job. In 1905 he received a patent for a tabulation machine, and in 1913 he invented a tallying machine. These machines made his work and the work of others at the Census Bureau much easier. Of course the Census Bureau workers of today use computers to help make their jobs easier, but in Pelham's time his machines were a great help.

Pelham's invention was not the only accomplishment of his lifetime. He was successful in other endeavors as well. He was born on a Petersburg, Virginia, farm in 1859. His parents owned their own farm which was a great accomplishment for an African American in those days. The Pelhams had worked hard to purchase the farm. When the white neighboring farmers saw that the Pelhams were becoming prosperous, they began to harass them. The Pelhams grew tired of this kind of treatment. They moved to Columbus, Ohio, and then to Philadelphia before finally settling in Detroit, Michigan. In Detroit, Robert went to school and worked as a newspaper boy delivering the *Detroit Post*. When he graduated from high school, he became a full-time worker at the newspaper. When he had learned enough about newspaper production, he and his brother published a small newspaper called the *Venture*. Later they began publishing a larger weekly newspaper called the *Plaindealer*. The *Plaindealer* became the leading African American newspaper in the Midwest. Some of the outstanding African Americans who contributed to the *Plaindealer* were Frederick Douglass, John Lynch, John Bruce, Blanche Bruce, and Ida Wells (Barnett).

Robert Pelham became a man of prosperity and influence. He also became involved in politics. He believed that African Americans could make better progress through their involvement in politics. Robert Pelham, Jr., acted on his belief. He gained influence in the Republican party and organized political clubs and organizations. In 1884 he was appointed a clerk in the Detroit Internal Revenue Office. In 1887 he became deputy oil inspector in Detroit. In 1888 he was a delegate to the Republican National Convention. In the 1880s and 1890s Pelham became a leading African American politician. He left his newspaper job and served full time in government positions.

After thirty-seven years of working at the U.S. Census Bureau, Pelham retired and published the *Tribune*, an African American newspaper, and started a news agency called the Capital News Service, Inc. While working at the Bureau, Pelham attended Howard University and received his law degree.

Robert Pelham died of a heart attack at his home in Washington, D.C., on June 12, 1943. He was buried in the Lincoln Memorial Cemetery. Robert Pelham had shown to the world that hard work and commitment are two things that lead to success and accomplishments.

"I Quote"

"Genius is one percent inspiration and ninety-nine percent perspiration." This statement was made by Thomas Edison. What do you think it means? Write your answer below.

Write a quotation based on the information given about Robert Pelham's life history.

On the two bumper stickers below give advice to a person who wants to be successful.

Explanation, Please!

The first United States census was taken in 1790. This information was used by the government to determine the amount of taxes that each state should pay and the number of congressional representatives each state was allowed. It took a year and a half to complete the census. Many people refused to cooperate because they did not know why the government wanted this information and what the information was going to be used for. Some people today still feel this way.

You are a government official. Your job is to explain to ordinary people what the U.S. Census Bureau is and what the information that it collects is used for. Use an encyclopedia or other reference books and write a page of information that you will use in your explanation.

The United States Census . . .

New and Improved

In 1913 Robert Pelham, Jr., invented a tallying machine. Research his machine; then design a machine that would be an updated improvement of Pelham's. Describe and draw a sketch of your machine below.

Dreaded Chores No More

If you are like most other students, making your bed and doing your homework are two most dreaded chores. In the spaces below draw and label a robot to do each chore.

A Machine That Makes Your Bed

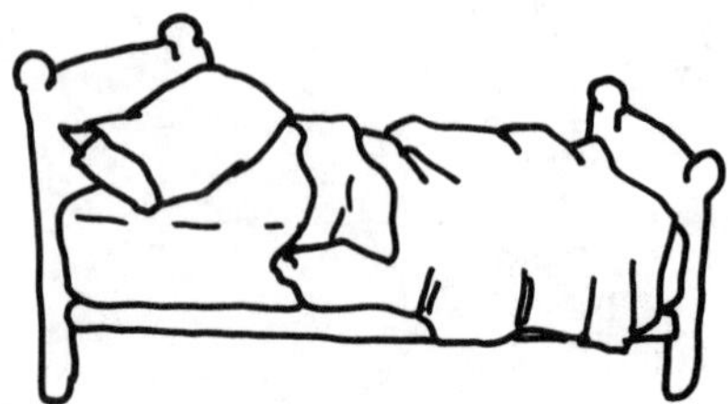

A Machine That Does Your Homework

On the back, list other "dreaded" chores and draw robots to do them too.

Elijah J. McCoy

Elijah J. McCoy
(1843-1929)
"The Real McCoy"

In 1870 Elijah McCoy became a very famous man. He started his own company to manufacture his new invention–the first automatic machine lubricating device called the "lubricator cup." In 1872 he was granted a patent for his invention. His lubricator cup allowed oil to drip continuously onto the moving parts of a machine while it was still in operation. Before McCoy's invention, machines had to be shut down before being oiled. His automatic lubricator cup was very important to industry because it saved time and money.

McCoy didn't just decide to invent his lubricator cup. He invented it because he saw a need for it. Here is the story. McCoy was born in Colchester, Ontario, Canada, in 1843. His parents had escaped as slaves and fled to Canada by way of the Underground Railroad. In Canada the McCoys longed for their son Elijah to get a good education. By the time Elijah was fifteen years old they had saved enough money to send him to Edinburgh, Scotland, to study engineering. When Elijah completed his studies there, he returned to the United States well trained and eager to go to work. But he was disappointed. Even though he was trained and educated, he could not find a good engineering job. He was repeatedly denied a job because he was African American. But Elijah was not to be outdone. He took a job as a fireman for the railroad. His job was to shovel coal into the train engine and stop the machine and oil it by hand. This is when Elijah began to think of a way to lubricate the engine while it was still running. He began to experiment, and finally he invented his lubricator cup.

Large industries in the U.S., Canada, and abroad began to request McCoy's invention. Everyone began bragging about having "the real McCoy," an expression that is still used today. Many people didn't know that such an ingenious device was invented by a black man. Sometimes they cancelled their order when they learned of Elijah's race, even though they needed his invention badly.

In 1929 Elijah McCoy died in Detroit, Michigan, at the age of 85. Today his lubricator cup is still being used in automobiles, locomotives, rockets, ships, and other machines. Elijah McCoy's invention will always be remembered as the revolutionary device that helped to modernize the industrial world.

Categorize It

People have invented since the dawn of time. Their inventions have caused many changes in our way of life.

Most inventions can be grouped into seven categories. The categories are listed on this page and the following page. Select inventions from the word bank and place them in the correct categories. Into which category would you put Elijah McCoy's invention? ________________

1. Inventions in Agriculture

____
____
____
____

2. Inventions in Communication

____
____
____
____

3. Inventions in Home and Family Life

____
____
____
____

4. Inventions in Medicine

____
____
____
____

5. Inventions in Science and Industry

____
____
____
____

Categorize It

6. Inventions in Transportation

____

____

____

____

7. Inventions in the Military

____

____

____

____

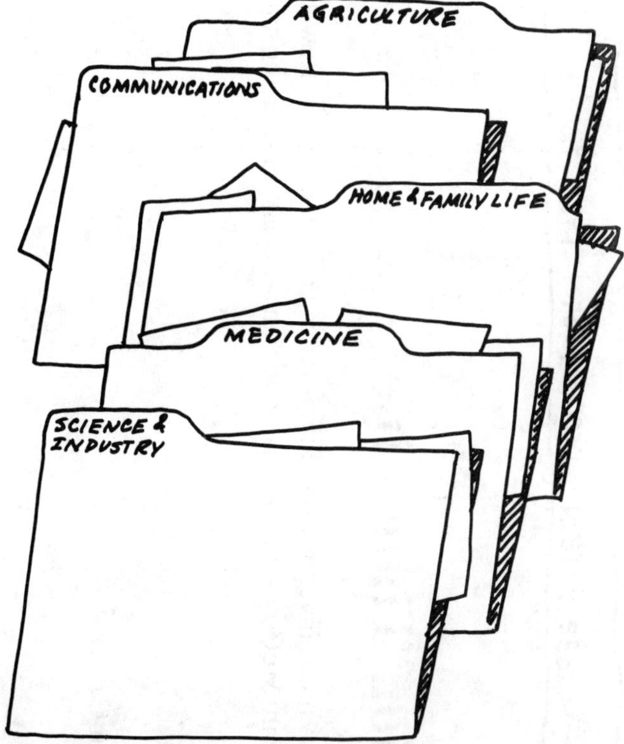

Word Bank

electric motor	gunpowder	stethoscope	vacuum cleaner
sewing machine	tractor	cotton gin	bicycle
radar	wheel	X ray	television
steam engine	pencil	radio	telescope
atomic bomb	thermometer	movies	refrigerator
barbed wire	plow	airplane	microscope
automobile	microwave oven	dynamite	laser

1753 1845 1846 1857 1872 1876 1883 1888 1891 1900 1904 1923 1990

Invention Time Line

Elijah McCoy invented his motor lubricator cup in 1872. Eleven more inventions and their dates are listed below. Rewrite the list so that the dates are in chronological order. Don't forget to include Elijah McCoy's invention. Place an asterisk beside the name of each African American inventor.

Invention	Inventor	Date
1. uses for peanuts	George Washington Carver	1900
2. safety pin	Walter Hunt	1846
3. telephone	Alexander Graham Bell	1876
4. radio	Lee de Forest	1888
5. sewing machine	Elias Howe	1845
6. tractor	Benjamin Holt	1904
7. toilet paper	Joseph Gayetty	1857
8. shoe last	Jan Matzeliger	1883
9. traffic light	Garrett Morgan	1923
10. clock	Benjamin Banneker	1753
11. big blue street mailbox	Phillip Downing	1891

Express It

Elijah McCoy's invention became so popular that people today use the expression "the real McCoy" to describe something that is genuine, original, or authentic.

Ten everyday expressions are listed below. Write what you think each means beneath the expression. On the back of this page, write ten more expressions and their meanings.

1. "I was down in the dumps."

____

2. "She is a couch potato."

____

3. "She was left holding the bag."

____

4. "He had egg on his face."

____

5. "People who live in glass houses shouldn't throw stones."

____

6. "If a man fools you once, shame on him; if he fools you twice, shame on you."

____

7. "Fish and kinfolks stink after three days."

____

8. "Do not put off for tomorrow what you can do today."

____

9. "Do unto others as you would have them do unto you."

____

10. "Don't put all your eggs in one basket."

____

Fun Inventions

The speedometer is a device to measure speed. It was invented to measure the speed of a traveling automobile. A ruler is used to measure the length, width, or height of something.

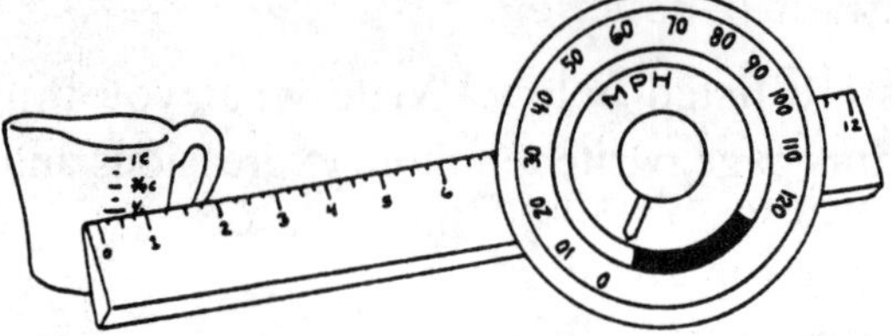

Use your imagination and invent a machine to measure the following. Write a detailed paragraph about each invention. Use the back of this sheet if you need more space.

1. A machine that shows how fast your parents get angry when you disobey

____

____

____

2. A machine that measures how fast a person talks

____

____

____

3. A machine that measures the amount of water that you drink each day

____

____

____

4. A machine that measures how much homework you have done

____

____

____

5. A machine that measures the number of hours that you watch television each week

____

____

____

Frederick McKinley Jones

Frederick McKinley Jones
(1892-1961)
Refrigeration Engineer

If you like your supermarket vegetables crisp and fresh with that "just-picked" taste, then you can thank Frederick McKinley Jones. His invention of a truck refrigeration system made it possible for foods to be hauled from farms to supermarkets across the country without spoilage.

Frederick, the genius inventor, was born in Cincinnati, Ohio, in 1892. He was orphaned at age 9. He had to quit school and work for a living. He had only a sixth grade education. Frederick was curious. He enjoyed taking things apart to see how they worked. When he was older, he enjoyed building, racing, and fixing sports cars.

Frederick first became known in the 1920s when he invented an inexpensive way to make silent movies "talk." In 1938 he received his first patent when he invented a machine to dispense tickets used in movies and theaters. In the late 1930s Frederick began to work on his most famous invention of all, a truck refrigeration system. One day the man for whom Frederick worked was playing golf with a friend who was a farmer. The farmer complained of losing money because truckloads of his farm vegetables sometimes spoiled before they reached the supermarkets and grocery stores. Frederick used old scrap parts and began to work on a way to keep the food from spoiling over long hauls across the country. When he had finished his invention, he tried it out and it worked. He attached the cooling system to a truck and voila–a truck refrigeration system. This meant that fresher fruits and vegetables could then be found in supermarkets and grocery stores.

The man for whom Frederick worked formed the Thermo Control Company to manufacture Frederick's invention. The company soon grew to be a three-million-dollar-a-year business. Frederick became vice president of the new company. His truck refrigeration system was soon placed in ships and railway cars. Today the same system is used in transporting rocket fuel.

When Frederick McKinley Jones died in Minneapolis, Minnesota, in 1961, he had sixty invention patents for his refrigeration equipment. The next time that you go to the supermarket to buy crisp, fresh vegetables, think of Frederick McKinley Jones. We could not enjoy such fresh foods if it were not for Frederick McKinley Jones' invention.

Food Stuff

Frederick McKinley Jones' invention of a truck refrigeration system made it possible for fruits, vegetables, meat, and dairy products to be shipped all over the country without spoilage. You can observe the degree of spoilage and changes in foods by doing the experiment below.

Place a small sample of the following foods in an aluminum pie pan. Put the pan of food samples outdoors in a place where they will not be disturbed. Observe the samples each day for a week. Record your observations and a description of each food sample in the chart below.

Name of Food Sample	Day 1	Day 2	Day 3	Day 4	Day 5	Day 6	Day 7
apple slice							
bread slice							
white potato slice							
orange slice							
food sample of your choice							

Which food showed the greatest change in a week? Which food showed the least change?

Test It!

Frederick McKinley Jones came up with his idea of inventing a truck refrigeration system when he overheard his supervisor discussing the problem of food spoilage. Frederick then thought of an air-conditioned truck that would keep foods from spoiling over long trips. How many ideas can you come up with to keep an ice cube from completely melting without using refrigeration? List your ideas. Put an asterisk beside your most clever idea. Select one idea from your list and write a plan or design to test it. Get your teacher's permission to test your idea. Complete the information below to show how you would test your idea.

Materials (what I need): ____

____

____

____

Procedure (what I will do): ____

____

____

____

Conclusion (what happened): ____

____

____

____

Write up your idea so that someone else could follow your directions and test your idea.

Preserve It!

Long before refrigeration, food was preserved by canning, curing, and drying. Research and write a paragraph telling how each is done.

Canning ____

____

____

____

Curing ____

____

____

____

Drying ____

____

____

____

Refrigeration and freezing are two of the most modern methods used to preserve foods. Make a list of ten or more foods that are found in your home freezer. Some foods cannot be frozen. Use a reference book or an encyclopedia to list foods that do not make good frozen products.

Have It Your Way

Most nations have foods that have become favorites among their people. You are a waiter for the "Have It Your Way" International Restaurant. There are ten plates on the table that represent places for people from ten different countries. Select foods from the microwave oven and place each on the correct plate.

Draw a centerpiece for the middle of the table with each country's flag represented.

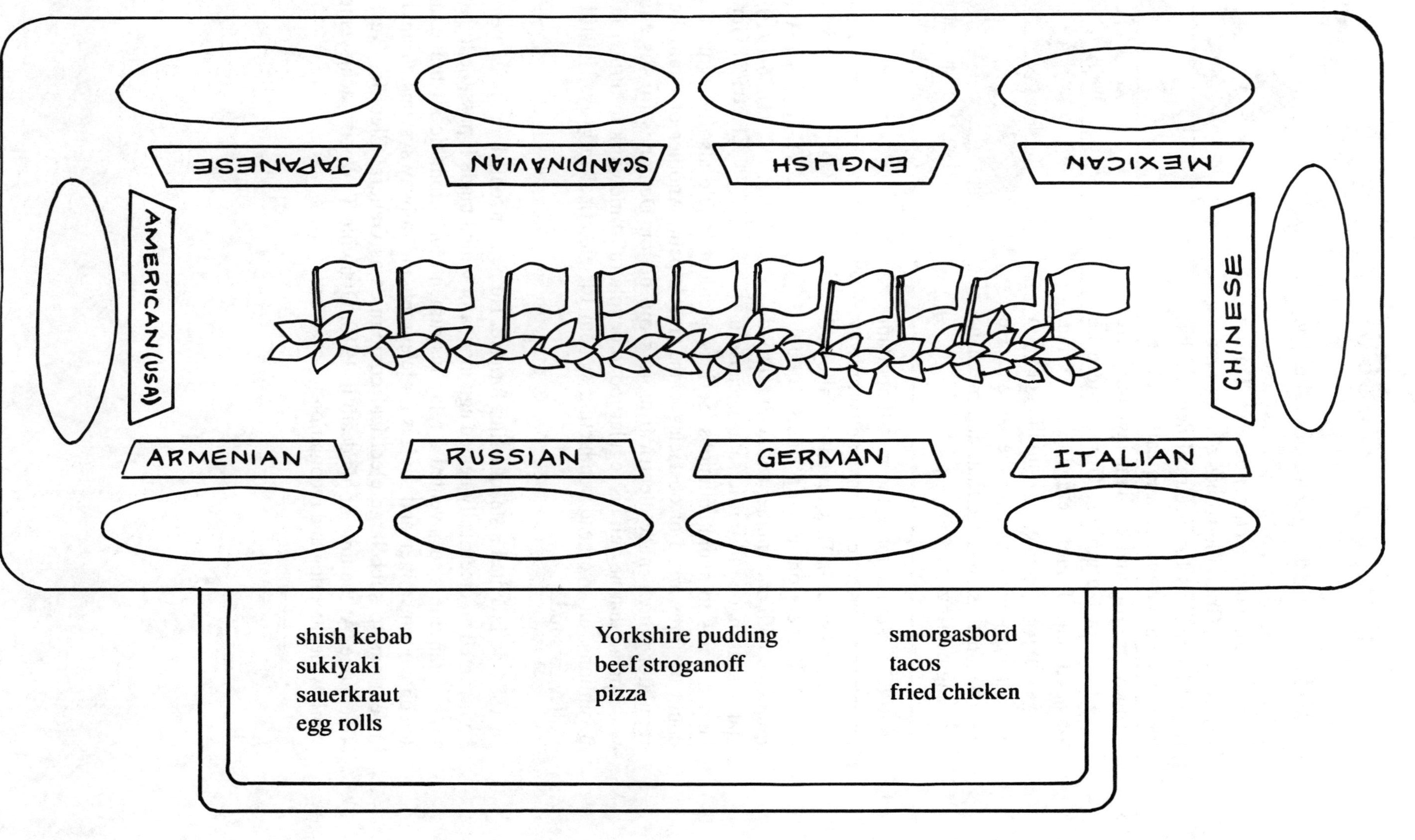

Granville T. Woods

Granville T. Woods
(1856-1910)
Electrical Genius

Granville T. Woods is sometimes called the "Black Thomas Edison" because he invented so many electrical devices. During his lifetime, Granville Woods obtained more than fifty patents for electrical devices that he invented. Granville was called an "extremely prolific and brilliant inventor." He was born in Columbus, Ohio, where he attended school until the age of ten. When he was sixteen years old, Granville got a job as a fireman-engineer with the railroad. He also began to study electrical and mechanical engineering.

In 1887 Granville made the most important invention of his time. He invented a railway telegraph system. This invention allowed crew members on moving trains to communicate with one another and with railroad stations. It made rail traffic safer because it helped trains to avoid collisions. Serious accidents could also be avoided because conductors could be forewarned of obstacles in the train's path. Another of Granville's inventions was a regulator which made electrical motors run better. Demands for his equipment became so widespread that he quit his regular job to devote full-time work to further inventions. One of his inventions, an overhead conducting system for electrical railways, is still used by trains and trolley cars today.

In 1884 he invented a steam boiler furnace. He next invented an amusement apparatus. In 1890 he invented an electrically heated egg incubator which made it possible to hatch 50,000 eggs at a time. Granville also invented a relay instrument, an automatic air brake, an electric battery, a telephone transmitter, and devices for telegraph and railway systems. Granville sold many of his inventions to such large electrical companies as General Electric, Westinghouse, and Bell Telephone. At the time of his death in 1910, Granville T. Woods' achievements had gained him worldwide attention and recognition.

Objects of Communication

Granville's most important invention was the railway telegraph system which allowed crew members on moving trains to communicate with one another, thus avoiding collisions and serious accidents.

There are many ways to communicate and many objects that help us to communicate. Twenty communication objects are hidden in the story below. Can you find them all? Circle the ones that you find.

The alarm clock rings, you jump out of bed, turn on the radio, and make up your bed. Your mother rings the breakfast bell and you go to the table for breakfast. Your dad speaks to you as he unrolls the morning newspaper. The phone rings. The microwave oven sends out a signal that your instant cereal is ready. The smell of coffee fills the house; the perk, perk of the coffeepot tells your mom that the coffee is ready. You finish your breakfast, dash back to your room, grab your books, glance at the wall clock, and race down the stairs. Your mother is in the car waiting. She honks the car horn. You get in the car and come to the traffic light at the end of the street. It is always red when your mother thinks it should be green. Just as the light changes you hear the siren of a police car rushing to the scene of an accident. You arrive at school just as the tardy bell rings. You slip into the classroom. The teacher calls the roll and gets started with the class. She picks up a piece of chalk and begins to write on the board. You are puzzled about what she is writing, but you pick up your pencil and begin to write. The girl next to you raises her hand and asks a question. The office buzzer gives the tornado signal. All your classmates file out of the room, drop to their knees, and cover their heads with their arms. When tornado drill is over, you go back to your classroom. The teacher turns on the television and puts in a video about whales. When the school day is over you rush home, turn on your compact disc (CD) player, and enjoy some soothing music to study by.

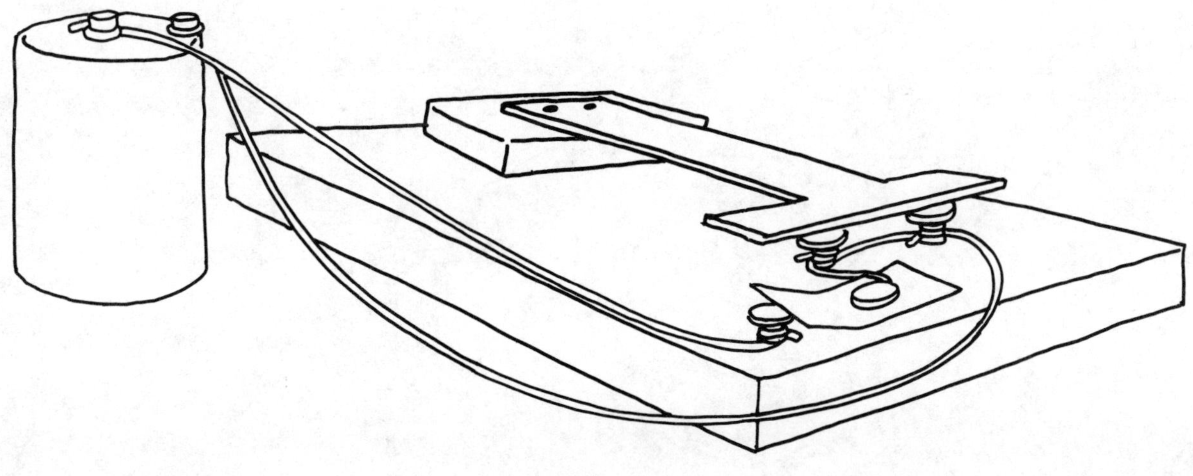

A–One, A–Two, A–Three

Dancing is one of the most personal forms of communication. In the 1980s Michael Jackson, the entertainer, singer, and dancer, created a performance dance called the "Moon Walk" in which he glided across the stage to the beat of his music.

Since dance is a form of communication and a way to express yourself, create your own dance that expresses who you are. Invent a new dance step in your routine and also design a costume that you would wear while performing your dance. Draw a full-color sketch of your costume below.

Household Inventions

Granville T. Woods invented many helpful devices that were used every day. Listed below are the names of twelve other African American inventors, the names of their inventions, and the dates of each invention. The story of how they came to invent these household inventions is missing. Select five inventions from the list, and on another sheet of paper, write an imaginary story telling how each was invented.

Inventor's Name	Invention	Date
A.P. Ashbourne	Biscuit cutter	1875
L.C. Bailey	Folding bed	1899
Sarah Boone	Ironing board	1892
R.N. Hyde	Carpet-cleaning compound	1888
W. Johnson	Eggbeater	1884
J.L. Love	Pencil sharpener	1895
L.P. Ray	Dustpan	1897
A.C. Richardson	Churn	1891
G.T. Sampson	Clothes dryer	1892
T.J. Stewart	Mop	1893
J.T. White	Lemon squeezer	1896
S.R. Scottron	Curtain rod	1892

1. The invention: ______________________ This is how it was invented.
2. The invention: ______________________ This is how it was invented.
3. The invention: ______________________ This is how it was invented.
4. The invention: ______________________ This is how it was invented.
5. The invention: ______________________ This is how it was invented.

Arrange the list of household inventions in chronological order.

Remember Me

Since the discovery of electricity, many electrical devices have been invented to make use of this great natural force. Granville Woods obtained more than fifty patents for his electrical devices. Sometimes we forget about the important role that electrical devices play in our lives. Completing the activity below will help us to remember.

List all of the electrical devices and appliances in each room of your home.

In the living room

1. ______________________ 6. ______________________
2. ______________________ 7. ______________________
3. ______________________ 8. ______________________
4. ______________________ 9. ______________________
5. ______________________ 10. ______________________

In the den or family room

1. ______________________ 6. ______________________
2. ______________________ 7. ______________________
3. ______________________ 8. ______________________
4. ______________________ 9. ______________________
5. ______________________ 10. ______________________

In the kitchen

1. ______________________ 6. ______________________
2. ______________________ 7. ______________________
3. ______________________ 8. ______________________
4. ______________________ 9. ______________________
5. ______________________ 10. ______________________

In the bathroom

1. ______________________ 6. ______________________
2. ______________________ 7. ______________________
3. ______________________ 8. ______________________
4. ______________________ 9. ______________________
5. ______________________ 10. ______________________

In other places such as the garage, basement, etc., give the number of electrical devices.

Name of place: ______________________ Number of electrical devices: ________

Name of place: ______________________ Number of electrical devices: ________

Name of place: ______________________ Number of electrical devices: ________

Paul Revere Williams

Paul Revere Williams
(1894-1980)
Outstanding Architect

When Paul Revere Williams was born in Los Angeles on February 18, 1894, his parents had no idea that their son would grow up to become one of the world's leading architects. As Paul grew up, his interest in building and constructing things was manifested in the toys that he played with. As a child he would spend long hours designing and constructing buildings and structures. His interest in architecture never left him. When he completed high school, he attended the University of Southern California and the Beaux Art Institute of Design. He was appointed to the National Monument Commission by President Calvin Coolidge. President Dwight Eisenhower appointed him to the National Housing Commission. The Disabled American Veterans commissioned him to design the famous "Grave of the Unknown Sailor" at Pearl Harbor. For this he became internationally known. He received a gold medal from the American Institute of Architects for excellence in his design of the Movie Corporation of America building in Beverly Hills. In 1953 he received the prestigious N.A.A.C.P. Spingarn Medal for excellence in the field of architecture. During his lifetime Paul Williams designed over four hundred private homes in his home state of California. Among them were homes for Cary Grant, Tyrone Power, Lucille Ball, and Frank Sinatra. One of his most elegant projects was the plush Beverly Wilshire Hotel in Beverly Hills, California.

He was associate architect in the planning of the Federal Customs Building in Los Angeles and the Los Angeles International Airport. He also designed the Arrowhead Hot Springs Hotel in San Bernardino, the Tennis Club at Palm Springs, the Saks Fifth Avenue store in Beverly Hills, and the Royal Nevada Hotel in Las Vegas. He was associate architect for the United Nations Building in Paris. As a gift, he designed the St. Jude Children's Research Hospital in Memphis, Tennessee.

Paul Revere Williams' work had a great influence on the world of architecture.

The Paul R. Williams Residence

Paul Revere Williams spent much of his life designing homes and buildings for others. Imagine that at the time of his retirement, he asked you to be the chief architect to design his retirement home in the Arizona desert. In the space below draw a sketch of the home that you will design for this great architect.

Outside Sketch

Inside Floor Plan

Animal Architect

Some animals are said to be great architects because of the painstaking care that they take in designing their homes. Research and complete the animal chart below. The first one has been done for you.

Name of Animal	Structure Built by Animal	Drawing of Structure
Spider	Web	
Beaver		
Prairie dog		
Earthworm		
Bird		
Wasp		

Select one animal from the chart and write a two-paragraph report on how it constructs its shelter.

Designing Architect

Architects design many different kinds of structures, from houses, schools, hotels, hospitals and stadiums to factories, monuments, churches, and even playground equipment.

Imagine that you have been commissioned by the recreation department of your city to design a new piece of playground equipment that would be fun for students your age. Follow the steps below to complete your design.

1. Glue the shape page (page 77) to a piece of construction paper. Let dry.
2. Cut out the shapes.
3. Arrange them into a three-dimensional standing design.
4. Display your structure on a piece of stiff cardboard or poster board.
5. Present your design to your classmates. To make your presentation more interesting, begin it with some background information about architecture. Use an encyclopedia to help you prepare your background information. Write what you will say in the space below.

Shape Patterns

Famous Architectural Structures

There are many famous architectural structures around the world. Some of them are listed in the chart below. Use an encyclopedia or other reference books to help you complete the chart.

Name of Structure	Location (city, country, etc.)	Architect or Designer	Additional Interesting Information
1. The Eiffel Tower			
2. The Lincoln Memorial			
3. The Taj Mahal			
4. The White House			
5. Notre Dame Cathedral			
6. The Pyramids			
7. Arc de Triomphe			
8. The Statue of Liberty			
9. Milan Cathedral			
10. The Parthenon			

George Washington Carver

Much is known about Dr. George Washington Carver's experiments that yielded many products from the peanut and sweet potato. But many people might not know that Dr. Carver was also an artist. He enjoyed painting pictures and crocheting.

George Washington Carver
(1860-1943)
Agricultural Chemist

George Washington Carver was born a slave in Missouri. He never knew his father. While he was still a baby, his mother was kidnapped by slave catchers, leaving little George orphaned. The Carvers, the white family who owned the plantation where George's mother worked, took George in. The Carvers noticed early that George was an extremely bright child so they helped him get a good education. When George was young, he spent many hours in the woods and gardens studying plants that grew there. At the age of eight, he was considered an expert on plants. Believing that he could learn more if he had a good education, George worked hard and completed high school. After his high school graduation, George wanted to go to college. He had excellent grades but because he was an African American, many colleges would not accept him. Finally, Simpson College in Iowa took him in. He was Simpson's first black student. After his college graduation he became a college teacher. He went to Tuskegee Institute (now Tuskegee University) in Alabama. While there he learned of the poor people and the poor soil that had been farmed the same way over the years. This one-crop farming had taken all of the nutrients out of the soil. Cotton was the only crop grown in the South. Dr. Carver introduced farmers to other crops and showed farmers the many uses and products of the peanut and potato. No one had ever thought of growing these crops. But Dr. Carver showed them that these crops could also be profitable. The farmers listened to Dr. Carver. They planted peanuts and sweet potatoes and soon these became two of the most important crops of the South.

For his experimentation and research, Dr. Carver gained international fame. People all over the world learned of this chemistry genius. Businesses and large research companies offered George large sums of money for his research and ideas but George was not interested. He could easily have been a very rich man but he wasn't interested in becoming rich. He just wanted to help humanity.

Dr. George Washington Carver won many honors and awards during his lifetime. People all over the world loved and respected this brilliant but humble man. When George Washington Carver died, the world mourned the loss of this great chemist. He left his life savings of $33,000 to establish the George Washington Carver Foundation to help provide research opportunities for other scientists. The George Washington Carver Museum on the Tuskegee University Campus has many of Dr. Carver's research products. On December 28, 1945, Congress declared that day as George Washington Carver Day. The farmland near Diamond Grove, Missouri, where Dr. Carver was born, is now a national landmark.

Other Uses

Dr. George Washington Carver invented hundreds of new ways to use the peanut and the sweet potato. You are an inventor. Invent a new use for each of the ten objects below. One is done for you.

Object	Original Use	New Use
1. A coat or jacket	to wear	as a rug
2. A toothbrush		
3. A book		
4. A pencil		
5. A lunch box		
6. A chair		
7. A ruler		
8. A clock		
9. A trash can		
10. A piece of bubble gum		

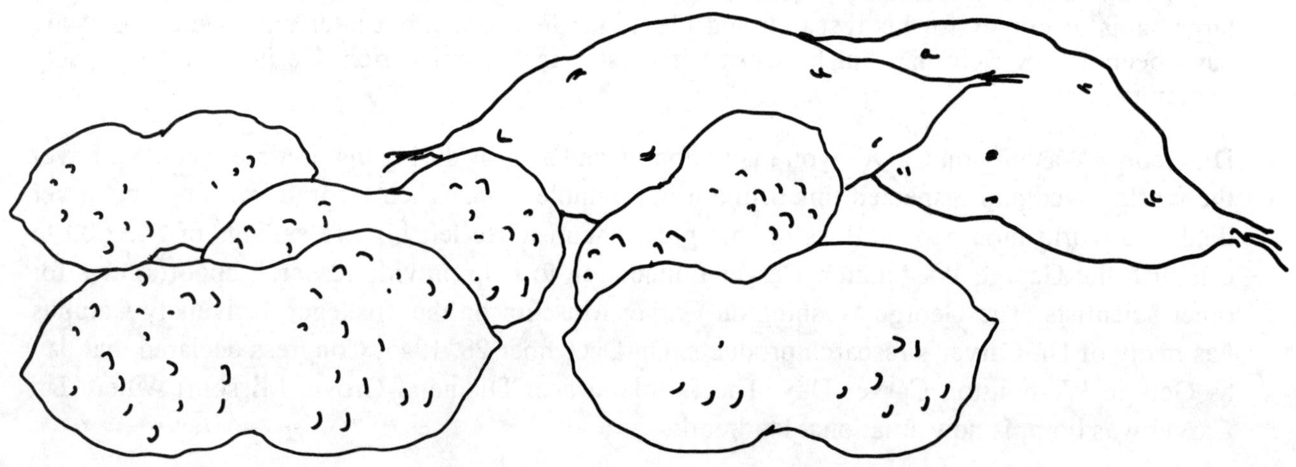

Sell It

The sweet potato is a popular food. Sweet potatoes may be yellow or white in color. They are a high energy food that contains two important vitamins, A and C. Suppose that you have just won a truckload of sweet potatoes in a "Sweet Potato Sweepstakes." What can you do with a truckload of sweet potatoes? You could sell them. Complete the storyboard below to write a television commercial to sell your sweet potatoes. Draw what will be seen in the squares and write what will be said on the lines. If you need to, consult reference books for more information on the sweet potato.

A Letter of Invitation

In the spring of 1896 Booker T. Washington, president of Tuskegee Normal and Industrial School, now Tuskegee University, wrote to Dr. Carver asking him to come to Tuskegee. In his letter he wrote ". . . I cannot offer you money, position, or fame. The first two you already have. The last you will no doubt obtain. I ask you to give up these things. I offer you in their place hard, hard work." Dr. Carver replied, "Of course, I will come. It has always been the one great ideal of my life to be the greatest good to the greatest number of people and to this end I have been preparing myself for these many years; feeling as I do that this line of education is the key to unlock the golden door of freedom to our people."

What famous person would you like to invite to your hometown? Complete the letters below.

Dear ______________________:
(name of famous person)

Please come to ______________________
(the name of your hometown or city)

to ______________________.
(give reasons why you want this person to come)

I cannot give you ______________________

but I can promise you ______________________.

Sincerely yours,

____
(sign your name here)

Now write a pretend response to your letter.

Dear ______________________:
(write your name here)

Of course I will come because ______________________

______________________.

Sincerely yours,

____
(sign the name of the famous person here)

Relationships

Listed below are words that are related to the many products that Dr. George Washington Carver produced from the potato, the peanut, the pecan, and cotton stalks. From the Word Bank below, select the product that is closely related to each word in the list and write it in the blank.

1. Pen ____________________
2. Hair ____________________
3. Bath ____________________
4. Biscuit ____________________
5. Sweet ____________________
6. Bean ____________________
7. Lipstick ____________________
8. Thinner ____________________
9. Carton ____________________
10. Oleomargarine ____________________
11. Sour ____________________
12. Lettuce ____________________
13. Iron ____________________
14. Rock ____________________
15. Cloth ____________________

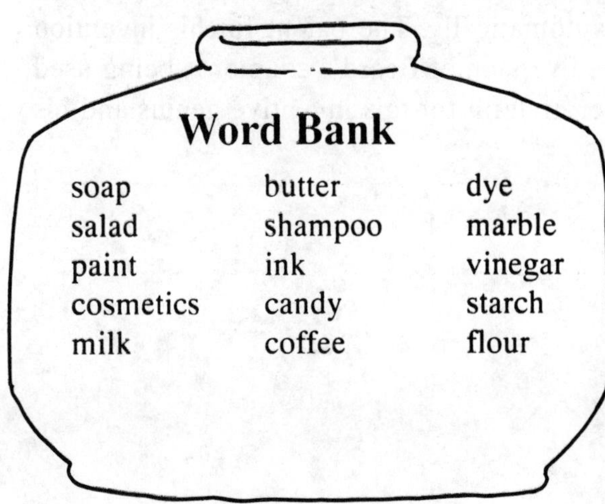

Word Bank

soap	butter	dye
salad	shampoo	marble
paint	ink	vinegar
cosmetics	candy	starch
milk	coffee	flour

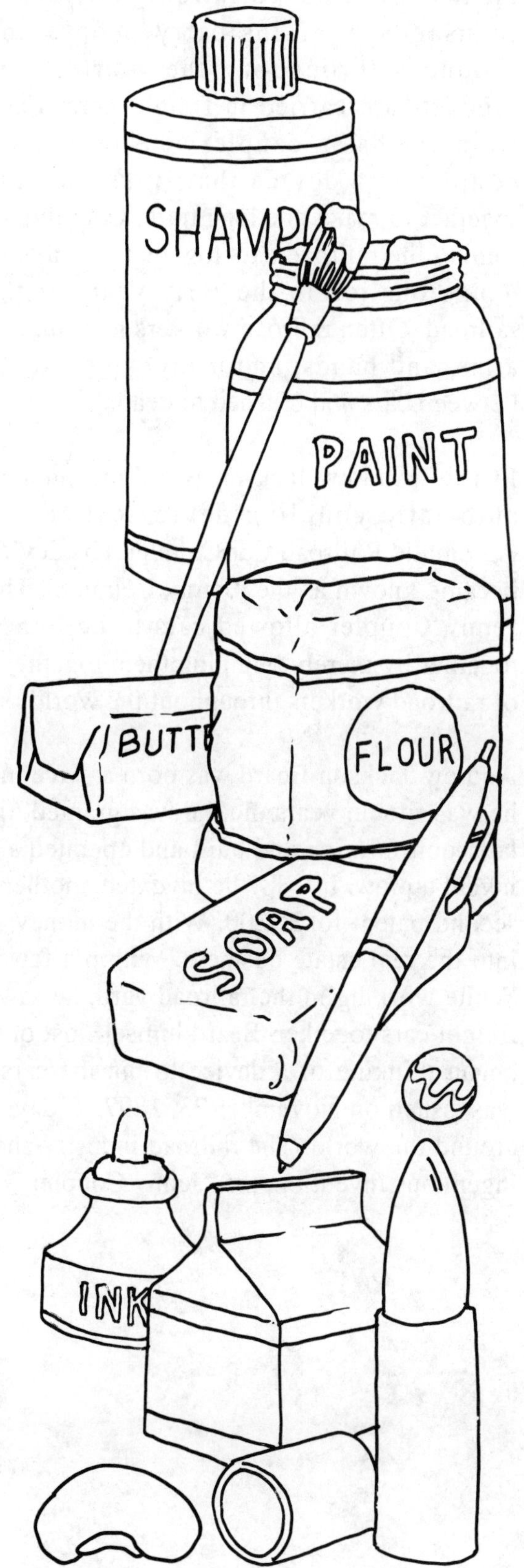

Andrew Jackson Beard

Andrew Jackson Beard
(1850-1910)
Inventor, Farmer, and Businessman

The railroad is one of our most important means of transportation. Each day thousands of trains carry people and products throughout the world. The products are carried in freight cars. Each train car has a coupler at each end. A coupler is a device that links the cars together to make one long train. Coupling or joining the railroad cars together was a very dangerous job in the early years of the railroad. Often railroad workers lost fingers, arms, and hands, and many were caught between cars and crushed to death.

In 1897 Andrew Jackson Beard invented an automatic coupling device called the Automatic Railroad Car Coupler. His device became known as the "Jenny Coupler." The Jenny Coupler allowed cars to be joined together by merely bumping them together. His invention saved the lives and limbs of thousands of railroad workers throughout the world.

Andrew Jackson Beard was born a slave in Jefferson County near Birmingham, Alabama. When he was fifteen years old, he was granted his freedom. He became a farmer for several years. He later quit farming and built and operated a flour mill. In 1881 he used his farming experience to invent a plow. In 1887 he invented another plow. He sold the first plow patent for $4000 and the second patent for $5200. With the money from his patents he bought houses and land and went into the real estate business. Within a few years Andrew Beard began working for the railroad. While working in the railroad yard, he saw several workers get injured while coupling (joining) freight cars together. Beard himself lost one of his legs during a train-coupling accident. He then began thinking of a device to pin the cars together automatically. The patent for his invention was issued on November 23, 1897. Today, an improved version of Beard's coupler is being used around the world. The railroad industry should be ever grateful for this inventive genius and his ingenuous invention, the "Jenny Coupler."

A Helping Hand

In 1897 Andrew Beard sold the patent to his invention, the Jenny Coupler, for $50,000. That was a sizeable sum in those days!

Research and write, in your own words, a half-page report on patents. Tell what a patent is and how to get one.

____

____

____

____

____

____

____

____

____

____

____

Suppose that you have won $50,000 in a "Helping Sweepstakes" in which you could keep $2000 for yourself and spend the remaining $48,000 helping others through the organization; then write the amount of the $48,000 that you would give each organization.

The United Way of America ____________________

The United Nation's Children's Fund (UNICEF) ____________________

The United Negro College Fund ____________________

The Salvation Army ____________________

The Red Cross ____________________

The Leukemia Society of America ____________________

The March of Dimes ____________________

The Nifty Fifty

What do you think are the fifty most interesting, important, and creative inventions of the past fifty years? Use research books such as *The World Almanac* and encyclopedias if you need help. List your answers in the spaces below.

1 ________	18 ________	35 ________
2 ________	19 ________	36 ________
3 ________	20 ________	37 ________
4 ________	21 ________	38 ________
5 ________	22 ________	39 ________
6 ________	23 ________	40 ________
7 ________	24 ________	41 ________
8 ________	25 ________	42 ________
9 ________	26 ________	43 ________
10 ________	27 ________	44 ________
11 ________	28 ________	45 ________
12 ________	29 ________	46 ________
13 ________	30 ________	47 ________
14 ________	31 ________	48 ________
15 ________	32 ________	49 ________
16 ________	33 ________	50 ________
17 ________	34 ________	

Safety Scientist

Andrew Beard can be called a safety scientist because his invention of the "Jenny Coupler" saved the limbs and lives of thousands of railroad workers.

Garrett Morgan is an African American inventor. He can also be called a safety scientist. Research and write about his two inventions and why they make him a safety scientist.

You Are

Andrew Beard was a businessman, farmer, and inventor.

Imagine you are each of the persons below and solve the problems in each space.

You are an inventor. Invent a new attractive door for your classroom. Draw your design.	You are an improver. What can you do to your car to make it the most exciting looking car on the block? Draw your improved car on the back of this sheet of paper.	You are a thinker. Think of 25 different uses for 10 large paper bags. Use the back of this sheet if you need more room.
You are a pet lover. What can you do to your dog to make it the cleanest and best-smelling dog in town? Write your ideas here.	You are a developer. Show how you would develop a one-acre plot of land to make a community that you would be proud of. Draw your community on a separate sheet of paper.	You are a designer. Design a wedding dress for a mouse. Draw it in the space below.

You are an advisor.

Your best friend's parents are getting a divorce. What advice can you give your friend?

Norbert Rillieux

Norbert Rillieux
(1806-1894)
Engineer and Inventor

Do you like to eat sweet snacks, caramel candy, or chocolate chip cookies? Then you can thank Norbert Rillieux for making it possible to buy such items at a reasonable cost. In 1846 Norbert Rillieux invented a vacuum pan that improved the method of making sugar from sugarcane. His invention reduced the cost of making granulated sugar. Before his invention, sugar was a luxury item that was used only on special occasions. His invention was hailed as one of the greatest inventions in the history of chemical engineering. It helped the United States to gain worldwide recognition in the sugar-refining business. Norbert Rillieux worked hard on his invention. He had tried and failed twice before finally devising his evaporation method. Norbert Rillieux's invention came into widespread use in Cuba, Mexico, and Europe. Yet because he was African American, he was not recognized in technical journals and science magazines as the other scientists were. A form of Norbert Rillieux's evaporator device is still being used today in the manufacturing of sugar, condensed milk, soap, gelatin, and glue.

It all began in 1806 when Norbert Rillieux was born in New Orleans, Louisiana, to a slave woman and a successful, wealthy, white engineer and plantation owner. His father sent him to Paris, France, to get an education. He then returned to New Orleans and made his famous invention.

Norbert Rillieux also invented a method to rid New Orleans of the mosquitoes that caused yellow fever. His plan was not accepted. Another group's plan which was almost exactly like Rillieux's plan was accepted. Rillieux became disgusted at the amount of prejudice against him because he was an African American. In 1854 he returned to France and became principal at a school that he once attended.

Rillieux died at the age of 88 and was buried in a churchyard cemetery in Paris, France. Thirty years after his death, Holland honored Rillieux for his sugar production invention. Soon afterwards, other countries began to honor him too. In 1934 Rillieux's home state of Louisiana finally honored him, and a bronze plaque was placed in his honor in the Louisiana State Museum.

Due Recognition

When Norbert Rillieux died in 1894 he still had not received the recognition that was due to him for such a revolutionizing invention. Imagine that the governor of Louisiana has appointed you to create four different items to honor Rillieux. Sketch designs of your items in the spaces below.

A car tag (license plate)

A postage stamp

A coin

A medal

Use the back of this page to write an article to your local newspaper about Norbert Rillieux. Give your article a title and begin writing.

List Them

Sugar is a common substance that is used as a sweetener. It is usually added to foods to improve their color, flavor, or taste.

Make a list of other substances that are added to foods to improve their flavor, color, texture (smoothness or roughness), or taste. Make your list as long as you can. Think! Think! Think! Combine your list with classmates to form a long class list. How many items can you list? How many different items can your entire class list?

1. ______________________________
2. ______________________________
3. ______________________________
4. ______________________________
5. ______________________________
6. ______________________________
7. ______________________________
8. ______________________________
9. ______________________________
10. ______________________________

Sweet Stuff

Norbert Rillieux's vacuum pan invention changed the color of sugar from its crude brown color to a refined white color. Some people did not like the white sugar because it was not its original brown color. Research the process of refining sugar and describe it below. Draw a flow chart to show the steps.

Sweetened Naturally

The governor of your state has declared war on cavities. Because sugar causes cavities, all uses of sugar are prohibited in your state. Tomorrow you and your family will have to get rid of all of the sugar and sweets in your house.

Research different artificial sweeteners and foods that contain natural sugar and list them below. Then find a recipe that uses a natural sweetener such as honey and write it below.

Benjamin Banneker

Benjamin Banneker (1731-1806) Outstanding Mathematician, Astronomer, Author, Surveyor, Humanitarian, and Inventor

In 1776 Benjamin Banneker said, "The color of the skin is in no way connected with strength of the mind or intellectual powers." Benjamin Banneker spent most of his life achieving and proving this statement to be true.

Benjamin Banneker was born near Baltimore, Maryland, in 1731. His mother was of mixed white and black ancestry and his father was African.

Benjamin lived all of his life on his parents' farm. He attended private schools and excelled in math. Schoolwork was easy for Benjamin. His two favorite subjects were math and science. His teachers were constantly looking for more difficult lessons for him. When he finished school he wanted to go to college but his parents did not have the money. As he grew older, he grew more curious about the things around him. One of the things that intrigued him the most was the stars. He was so fascinated by the stars that he adopted a rather strange life-style. He stayed awake and studied the stars at night and slept during the day. One day a man learned that Benjamin liked to study the stars, and he gave Benjamin a book on astronomy. The book told of the stars and planets. Benjamin read and studied the book until he became an expert in astronomy.

Benjamin soon became interested in another project. Once a traveling salesman showed Benjamin a pocket watch. Benjamin was so fascinated with it that the man gave it to him. Benjamin spent days taking it apart and learning about the workings inside. Using the watch as a guide, Benjamin invented the first clock ever to be built in America. His clock kept accurate time, striking every hour for more than forty years. News about the clock traveled fast. People came from all over the world to see it and the genius who invented it.

Benjamin became famous again in 1791 when President George Washington appointed him to help plan the city of Washington, D.C. He became the first black to be appointed to a job by a President of the United States. The original planner, Pierre L'Enfant, argued with federal officials and quit the job, carrying the original plans with him. All was lost, so the federal officials thought. But Benjamin Banneker had memorized the plans. He carefully drew the plans again for the great city. Benjamin helped select the present-day sites for the capitol buildings, the U.S. treasury building, the White House, and other federal buildings.

In 1792 Banneker began another project for which he gained great fame. He began writing an almanac. The almanac was filled with facts about the planets, the moon, and the weather. It also contained recipes, medical remedies, poems, and other useful information. It was the first scientific book ever written by an African American. His almanac became famous.

On October 25, 1806, Benjamin Banneker died while wrapped in a blanket, observing the stars. He had been living proof that "the color of the skin is in no way connected with strength of the mind."

Problems, Problems, Problems

Throughout his life, Benjamin Banneker loved to make up and solve math problems. Make up ten math problems. They can be reading problems or numerical problems. Write your math problems in the space below and write the solutions on the back of this sheet. When you have finished, exchange papers with a friend and try to solve each other's math problems without looking at the answers.

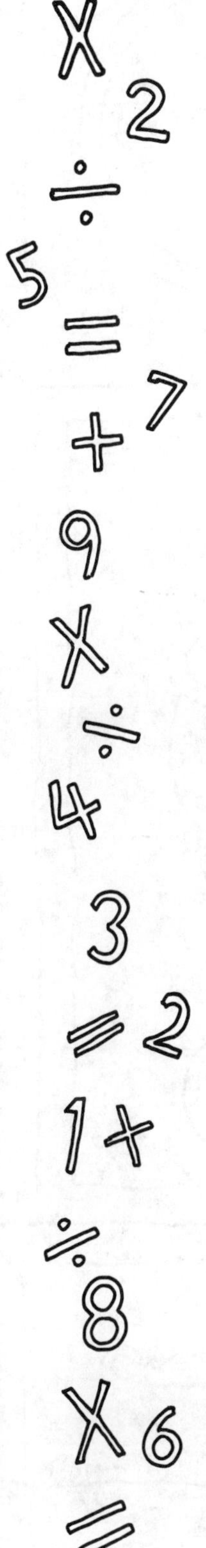

A Timepiece to Treasure

Today there are many kinds of clocks and watches. Some play tunes, run backwards, and have alarms. Design your own unique clock or watch. Give a detailed description of the timepiece and its functions. Draw a picture of your own clock or watch below.

Star Completion

Benjamin Banneker spent many nights gazing at the stars and constellations.

Read information from an encyclopedia about stars and constellations. Fill in each blank with the correct word from the Word Bank.

A ________________ (1) is a huge ball of hot, glowing gas in the sky. A star is made up of two gases, ________________ (2) and ________________ (3). People have studied stars since ancient ________________ (4). Early farmers watched the stars to know when to plant their ________________ (5). Travelers used stars to tell ________________ (6). Ancient people saw pictures in groups of stars. These groups of stars are called ________________ (7). Some star-like objects that we see in the sky are not called stars. There are nine of them and they are called ________________ (8). A binary star is two stars ________________ (9) around each other. Stars are not spread out evenly throughout the universe. They are clustered together in large groups of billions of stars called ________________ (10). An instrument that scientists use to study stars is called a ________________ (11). The size of a star varies. The largest stars are called ________________ (12). The smallest stars of all are called ________________ (13) stars. The ________________ (14) is a star. It is about 93 million miles (150 million kilometers) away from the earth. The distance between stars is measured in a unit called the ________________ (15). The study of stars, planets, and other heavenly bodies is called ________________ (16). The big and little ________________ (17) are constellations that are formed in the northern sky. Some constellations are named after ________________ (18) and some are named after ________________ (19) creatures. ________________ (20) is the name of a constellation.

Word Bank

neutrons	star	supergiants
helium	telescope	hydrogen
constellations	sun	times
revolving	crops	directions
light-year	planets	galaxies
dippers	astronomy	mythological
Orion	animals	

Math Plans

Benjamin Banneker used his math skills to help survey and lay out plans for the city of Washington, D.C. Use your surveying skills to draw a floor plan of your room. Pretend that you are looking down from the ceiling and draw the outline of your room. Make the drawing the same shape of your room–square, rectangular, round, etc. Label the closets, windows, and doors. Show the location of pieces of furniture–bed, dressers, desk, bookshelves, toy chest–whatever is in your room. You can use blocks, circles, and rectangles to represent things. Label each furniture piece. Be sure to include the dimensions–length and width–of your room.

Ask a member of your family to show you the plans for your house or apartment. Use the plans to draw a miniature version of each floor of your house or apartment. Show rooms, stairs (if any), doors, and windows. Show where pieces of furniture are located. Put in the dimensions of each room. Use the back of this sheet.

Louis Wade Sullivan

Louis Wade Sullivan
(1933-   )
Secretary of U.S. Department of Health and Human Services

In 1989 Dr. Louis Wade Sullivan became the highest-ranking African American in the administration of President George Bush. As the United States Secretary of Health and Human Services, Sullivan was the only black Cabinet member and managed the largest spending budget of any federal agency. When Dr. Sullivan was appointed to head the department of Health and Human Services, he began planning ways to improve the health of the nation. He worked to get more money for scholarships and research in the medical field.

Louis Wade Sullivan was born on November 3, 1933, in Atlanta, Georgia. He was the youngest of two sons born to Walter Sullivan, an undertaker, and Lubvida Sullivan, a school teacher. In his early childhood, his father moved the family to the country town of Blakely, Georgia. They later found that the small town did not offer the kind of educational opportunities that they wanted their children to have. So, they sent their sons back to Atlanta to live with friends and to attend school there.

The boys were taught to succeed and they did. Louis graduated from high school with honors and went on to Morehouse College, a primarily black college in Atlanta. He graduated with honors there and won a scholarship to study medicine at Boston University. In order to get the extra things that he needed, Louis worked as a waiter in a local restaurant. Louis worked hard and studied hard. His hard work and studying paid off. He graduated third in his class from Boston University Medical School. A string of successes followed for Louis. He began a teaching career which took him to Harvard Medical School, New Jersey College of Medicine, and back to his alma mater, Boston University. By this time Dr. Louis Sullivan had become a well-known hematologist. (A hematologist is a doctor who specializes in the treatment of blood diseases.)

When he was 42 years old, Dr. Sullivan dreamed of establishing a medical school at Morehouse College. In 1975 Dr. Sullivan headed a two-year medical college which later became a regular four-year medical program. Establishing of a good medical school took a great deal of time, but Dr. Sullivan succeeded. The Morehouse Medical School became one of only three primarily black medical schools in the United States. Meharry Medical College in Nashville, Tennessee, and Howard University Medical School in Washington, D.C., are the other two medical schools. Together they train the greatest number of black doctors in the United States.

Heads Up

The President's Cabinet is made up of the heads of executive offices in the federal government. These heads are called secretaries. Today there are fourteen such positions. These are listed below. Use an almanac, encyclopedia, or other reference books and write some information about each Cabinet position in each post below. Put an asterisk beside the post to which Dr. Louis Sullivan was appointed. Write the name of at least one person who has served or is serving in each position today.

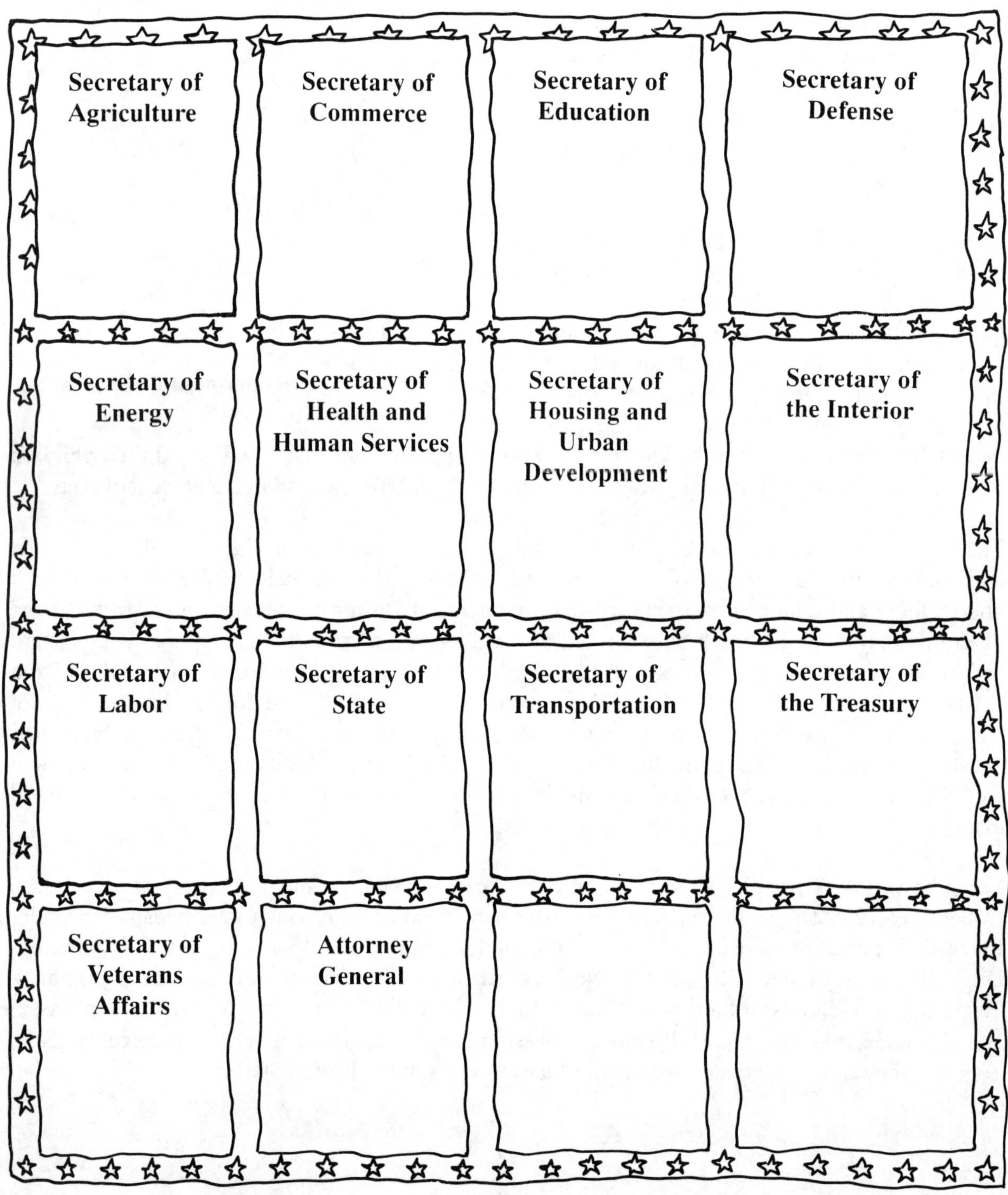

Post Officers

When Dr. Louis Sullivan became U.S. Secretary of Health and Human Services, he became the second African American to hold this Cabinet post. The first to hold the position was Patricia Harris, who held the office from 1979 to 1981 under President Jimmy Carter. In 1966 Robert Weaver became the first black Cabinet member in the history of the United States. He was appointed by President Lyndon Johnson. These African Americans were not the first to serve in high-ranking federal government positions. When Franklin Roosevelt was elected President in 1932 he expanded the federal government to include more African Americans. He appointed consultants to advise and inform him. These consultants were experts in their own areas. Many were college-educated, professional men and women. One of these consultants was Walter White; another was Lester Walton. Other African Americans who participated in the government were Mary McLeod Bethune and later Ralph Bunche, Arthur Mitchell, Oscar De Priest, Adam Clayton Powell, and William Dawson. The appointment and election of these early government officials paved the way for those that followed in more recent years. Today African Americans serve in almost every phase of government and continue to prove the leadership abilities of African Americans.

Use an encyclopedia or another reference book to write a factual sentence about each of the following:

1. Patricia Harris ____

____

2. Robert Weaver ____

____

3. Walter White ____

____

4. Lester Walton ____

____

5. Mary McLeod Bethune ____

____

6. Ralph Bunche ____

____

7. Arthur Mitchell ____

____

8. Oscar De Priest ____

____

9. Adam Clayton Powell ____

____

10. William Dawson ____

____

Take a Stand

As Secretary of the Department of Health and Human Services, Dr. Louis Sullivan was concerned about hazards to the health and well-being of every United States citizen. In such a position he had to think through and examine all sides of a health issue. Then he had to take a stand for it or against it. How do you stand on the following issues?

Read each issue carefully. Think about it. Then take a stand by circling *Yes* or *No* on the left side. Give two reasons for your answer on the right side.

1. Should animals be used in medical experiments?

Yes No	Reasons: 1. ______________________ 2. ______________________

2. Should tobacco and alcohol companies use athletes to advertise their products?

Yes No	Reasons: 1. ______________________ 2. ______________________

3. Should the U.S. have a national health system in which doctors are paid a modest fee by the government and medical care for every citizen is free?

Yes No	Reasons: 1. ______________________ 2. ______________________

4. In some school systems, students are given special places and times for smoking cigarettes. Do you think this is a good idea?

Yes No	Reasons: 1. ______________________ 2. ______________________

5. Should beer and wine commercials be shown on television?

Yes No	Reasons: 1. ______________________ 2. ______________________

6. Should federal money be used to build projects like space stations instead of being used for projects like building homes for the homeless?

Yes No	Reasons: 1. ______________________ 2. ______________________

Research one of the issues and give a report to the class.

Committed

Dr. Louis Sullivan said that he was committed to "ending America's love affair with cigarettes."

What do you think he meant by that statement?

What do you think is a good way to do this?

Complete the business letter to the current secretary suggesting ways to end "America's love affair with cigarettes."

__________, Secretary
U.S. Department of Health and Human Services
200 Independence Avenue, S. W.
Washington, D.C. 20201

Sincerely,

Be sure to use the correct business letter form. Share your letter with the class.

Charles Henry Turner

Charles Henry Turner
(1867-1923)
Scientist

To most people a cockroach is one of the most disgusting insects of all, but to Charles Henry Turner it was just another interesting insect to be studied. As a boy, Charles was always curious about insects. Every day he could be found watching and observing insects and writing down their behavior and the ways that they reacted with their environment.

One of his favorite insects to watch was the ant. Charles would lie on the ground watching the ants as they moved to and from their anthill home. He noticed that the ants sometimes traveled far from their homes, but they never got lost. This made Charles very curious about how the ants found their way back home. In observing the ants' behavior he discovered that ants use light rays to guide them in finding their way back to the anthill. In an experiment he put the ants in a container and removed the light from one side. When he did, the ants were confused. They panicked and acted lost. When he returned the light, the ants moved toward the light and reacted in a calmer manner. His work with ants and other insects made him an authority in the field of insect behavior.

Charles was born in Cincinnati, Ohio, in 1867. His father was a church custodian and his mother was a nurse. Charles' father loved to read. He collected hundreds of books. Charles also shared this love of reading, and he was fortunate to have many books from which to read.

When Charles completed high school, he attended the University of Cincinnati. After his college graduation, he began to devote his time to research in the area of entomology, studying the behavior of insects. In 1907 he earned a Ph.D. degree from the University of Chicago in animal (insect) behavior.

When Dr. Charles Turner died in 1923, the world lost a man of much intelligence. Dr. Turner did not work out of an expensive laboratory with new and great equipment. He used his five senses and made his discoveries with a small salary and a bright mind. Dr. Turner made many original discoveries, all because of his love for and dedication to his work in insect behavior.

Insect "Myth"ology

Insects are among the most fascinating animals on earth. Dr. Charles Turner and others who have studied them have found many startling facts about insects. Listed below are some statements. If you think the statement is a myth or is not true, place an M in front of it. If you think that it is true, place a T in front of it.

1. __________ Insects can smell with their antennae.
2. __________ Insects can taste with their feet.
3. __________ Insects cannot hear.
4. __________ Insects do not have voices.
5. __________ Insects can make noises that can be heard up to one mile away.
6. __________ Insects breathe with tiny lungs.
7. __________ Some insects have as many as five eyes.
8. __________ An ant can lift fifty times its weight.
9. __________ Some insects build tiny bridges and apartments.
10. __________ Some insects raise crops.
11. __________ A spider is an insect.
12. __________ Some insects go to war against one another.

Research and make an insect booklet called "Fascinating Facts About Insects."

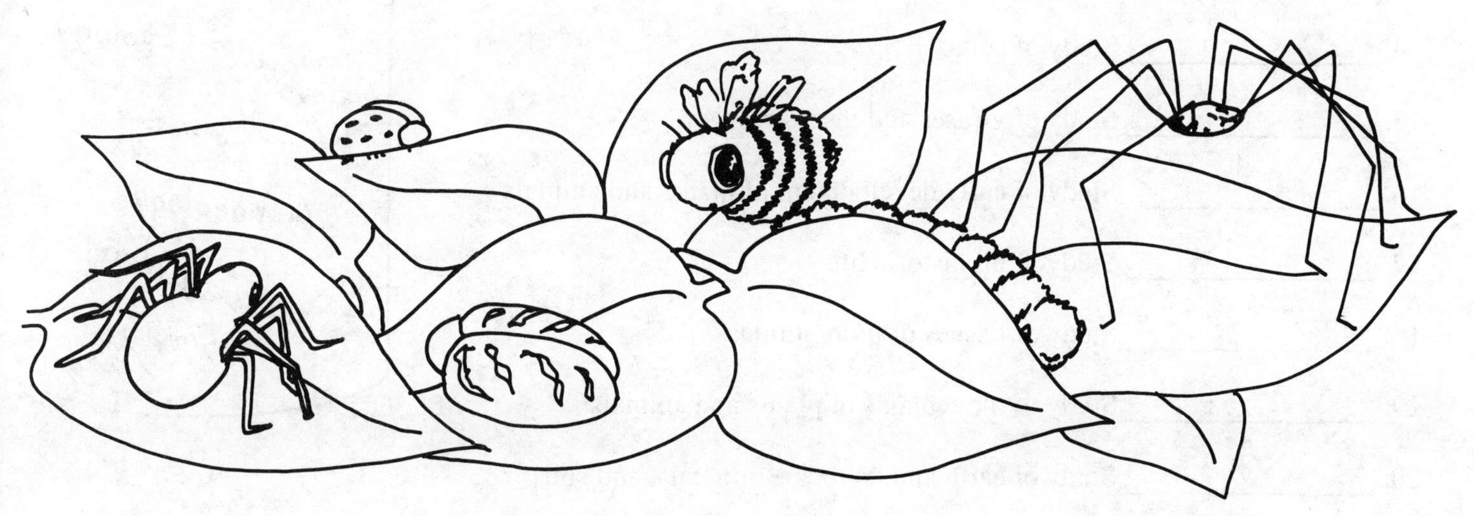

Other "Ologies"

Dr. Charles Turner loved to study insects. The study of insects is called entomology and a person such as Charles who studies insects is called an entomologist. There are other "ologies" that tell what scientists study.

Select the correct "ology" from the "ology" tank on the right and place it beside the correct phrase on the left.

1. _______________ Study of birds
2. _______________ Study of fish
3. _______________ Study of animals
4. _______________ Study of all living things
5. _______________ Study of how living things relate to their environment
6. _______________ Study of reptiles and amphibians
7. _______________ Study of mosses
8. _______________ Study of grasses
9. _______________ Study of fungi
10. _______________ Study of function of living things
11. _______________ Study of weather
12. _______________ Study of bacteria
13. _______________ Study of organisms that can only be seen with a microscope
14. _______________ Study of cells
15. _______________ Study of viruses and diseases
16. _______________ Study of early development of plants and animals
17. _______________ Study of prehistoric life
18. _______________ Study of tissues of living things
19. _______________ Study of the remains of plants and animals
20. _______________ Study of earth and its rocks, minerals, and soil

Histology
Virology
Zoology
Meteorology
Geology
Ichthyology
Cytology
Bryology
Biology
Ornithology
Graminology
Bacteriology
Mycology
Paleontology
Ecology
Herpetology
Physiology
Archaeology
Microbiology
Embryology

Insect Experiment

Dr. Charles Turner made many original insect discoveries. He found that bees memorize the area around their homes so that they do not get lost when they return. He also discovered that honey bees can distinguish between colors and patterns, and he learned that young cockroaches can learn.

You are Dr. Charles Turner's assistant. Your special project is to design a test or experiment to prove that moths prefer light to darkness. Use the outline below to design your experiment.

Title of Experiment ____

Equipment or Materials Needed __________________________________

Procedure (what you will do) ___________________________________

____

____

With your teacher's permission, try your experiment at home or school and write your results or conclusions (what you have learned) below.

____

____

____

____

____

____

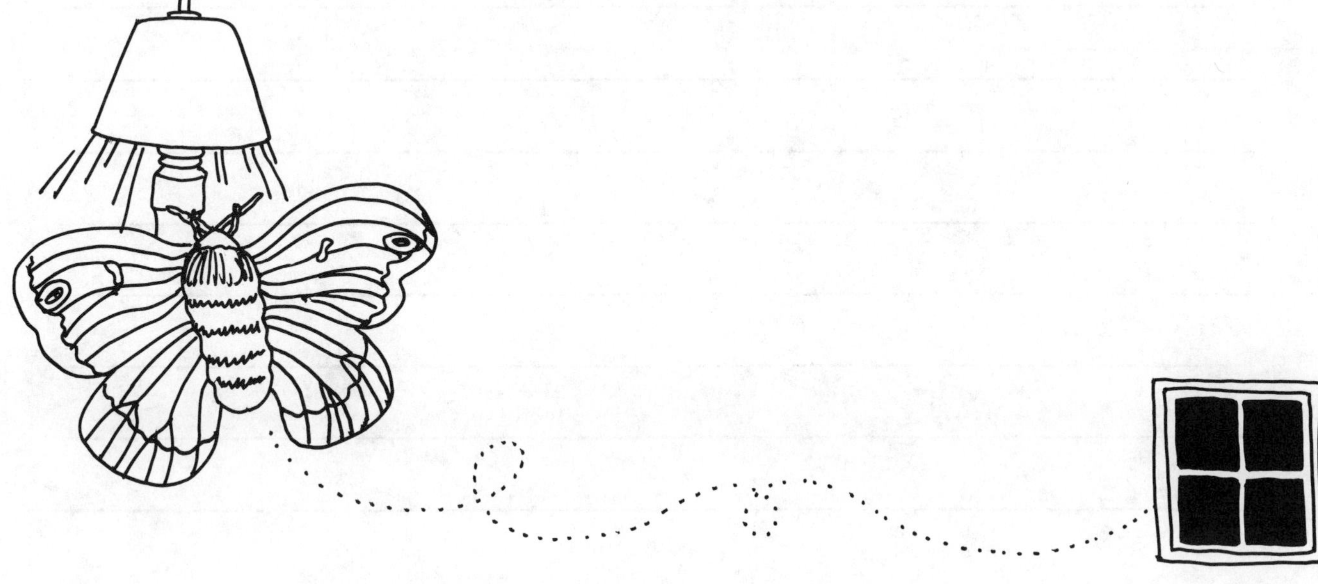

Killer Bees

Many stories, movies, and books have been written about insects. Most of the films about insect attacks are fictitious. Use your creative ability and write a good story about the time that killer bees came to your hometown. Make your story as interesting as possible.

The Day That the Killer Bees Came to ______________________________
(write the name of your hometown here)

Jan Ernst Matzeliger

Shoes come in almost every style, fabric, and size. They are an important part of people's attire. Over 265 million shoes are produced in the United States each year.

Despite the many changes in shoe styles, shoemaking itself has not changed much over the years. At first, shoes were handmade by skilled workers. These artisans worked slowly, producing only a few pairs of shoes at a time. This made the price of shoes extremely high.

Jan Ernst Matzeliger
(1852-1889)
The "Sole Man"

As expensive as shoes are today, they would be even more expensive if it had not been for Jan Matzeliger's invention. In 1882 he invented the shoe-lasting machine. This machine stitched the upper part of the shoe to the sole or bottom of the shoe. This led to the mass production of shoes and greatly reduced their prices.

Jan Matzeliger was born in Paramaribo, Suriname (Dutch Guiana), in 1852. His mother was a Black of Suriname and his father was an educated Dutch engineer from a wealthy and aristocratic family in Holland. When Matzeliger was 19 years old he came to America and worked in a shoe factory in Lynn, Massachusetts. Lynn was one of the leading shoe manufacturing centers in the nation. Matzeliger got a job at the Harney Brothers Shoe Manufacturing Company. While working in the factory, Matzeliger noticed the slow and tedius work of the shoemakers working by hand. For ten years, Matzeliger secretly began working on a machine that he thought would do the job much faster. First he made a wooden machine, then an iron one. In 1882 he revealed his new machine and sent his diagrams to Washington, D.C. In 1883 he was issued a patent for his machine. He did not have enough money to produce and sell his machine himself, so in 1885 he sold the patent to a company in Lynn which later became the United Shoe Machinery Company. His invention made Lynn, Massachusetts, the shoe capital of the world.

In 1889 Jan Matzeliger died of tuberculosis at the age of 37. He had received only a part of the profit that resulted from his invention.

On May 16, 1967, the city of Lynn honored its outstanding 19th century inventor. May 16 was declared Jan E. Matzeliger Day. Today's shoemaking factories still use machines very similar to the Matzeliger original.

The Daily Tell

On May 16, 1967, the city of Lynn, Massachusetts, honored Jan Matzeliger for his invention of the shoe-lasting machine.

You have entered a time machine and have been transported back to the year 1967 in Lynn, Massachusetts. You are a news reporter for *The Daily Tell* newspaper. You are covering the 1967 Jan E. Matzeliger Day celebration. Look around you. What do you see? Parades? Bands? In the newspaper below, tell it all.

Use an almanac to find out about other events that happened in 1967 (who was President of the U.S., etc.).

Shoe Award

In the shoe below design an award certificate to be presented to Jan Matzeliger for his shoe-lasting machine.

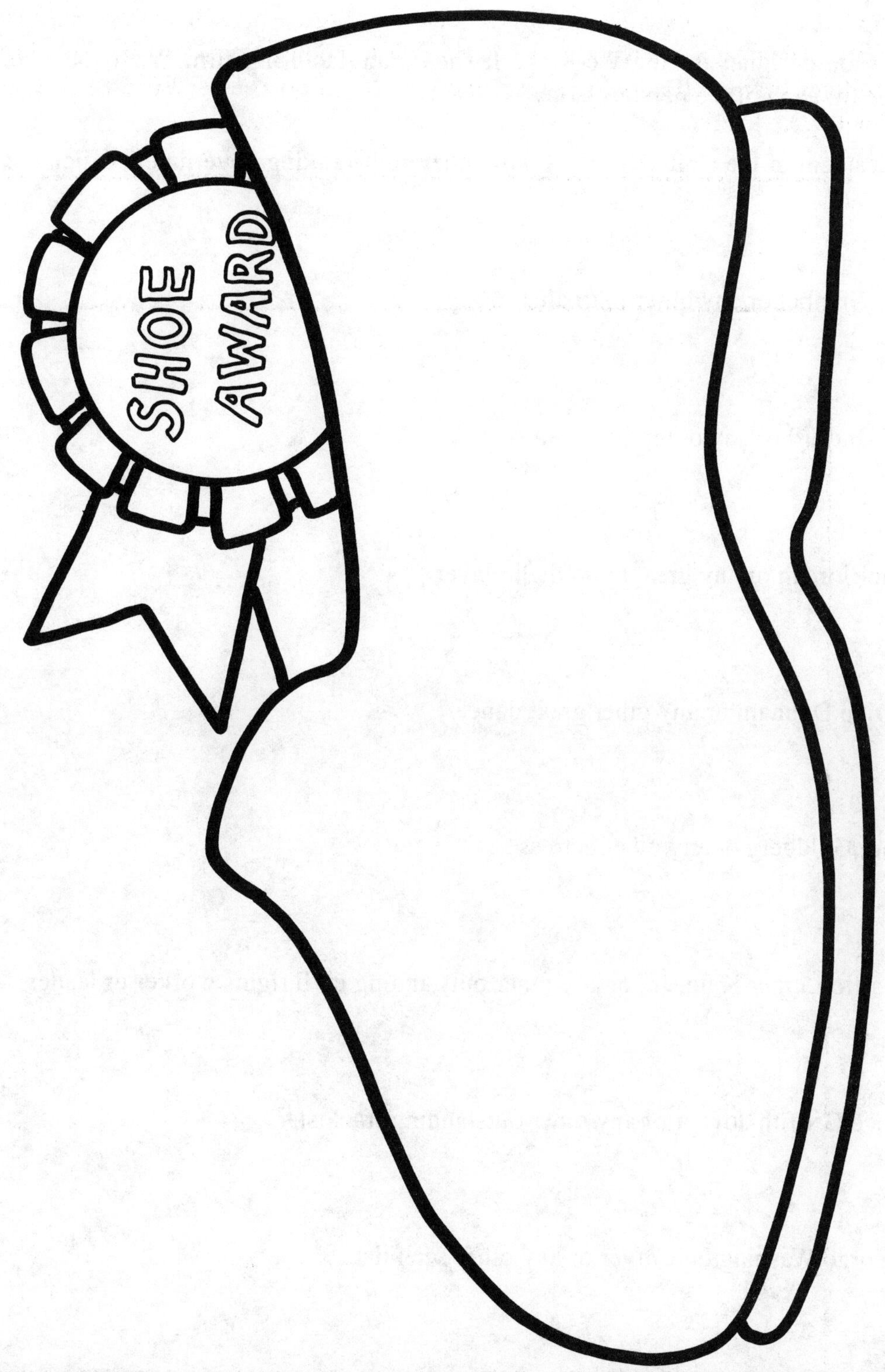

Design a trophy or a blue ribbon to be presented at a Jan Matzeliger celebration.

If the Shoe Fits

Throughout history, shoes have been worn not only for protection but also for decoration and to indicate social status. Sometimes movie stars and other persons of importance have their shoes designed especially for them.

You are a shoe designer for the We-Make-It shoe manufacturing firm. Your job is to design a unique shoe for each of the persons below.

1. The President of the United States or any other high-ranking government official

2. Bryant Gumbel or any other journalist

3. Guion Bluford or any other astronaut

4. Michael Jordan or any great basketball player

5. Katherine Dunham or any other great dancer

6. Whoopi Goldberg or any other actress

7. Dr. Martin Luther King, Jr., or any other outstanding civil rights worker or leader

8. Florence Griffith-Joyner or any other outstanding track star

9. Dr. George Washington Carver or any other scientist

10. M. C. Hammer or any other rap singer

The Shoe Is on the Right Foot

These African American scientists and inventors were attending a meeting together. They grew tired and removed their shoes. The shoes got all mixed up under the table. Help each person find his or her shoe by drawing a line from his or her name to the correct shoe. The hint on each shoe will help you. If you need more help, use encyclopedias or any other reference books.

1. Frederick Jones
2. Benjamin Banneker
3. Charles Henry Turner
4. Jennie Patrick
5. Percy Julian
6. Jan Matzeliger
7. Reatha Clark King
8. Jane C. Wright
9. George Washington Carver
10. Charles Bolden

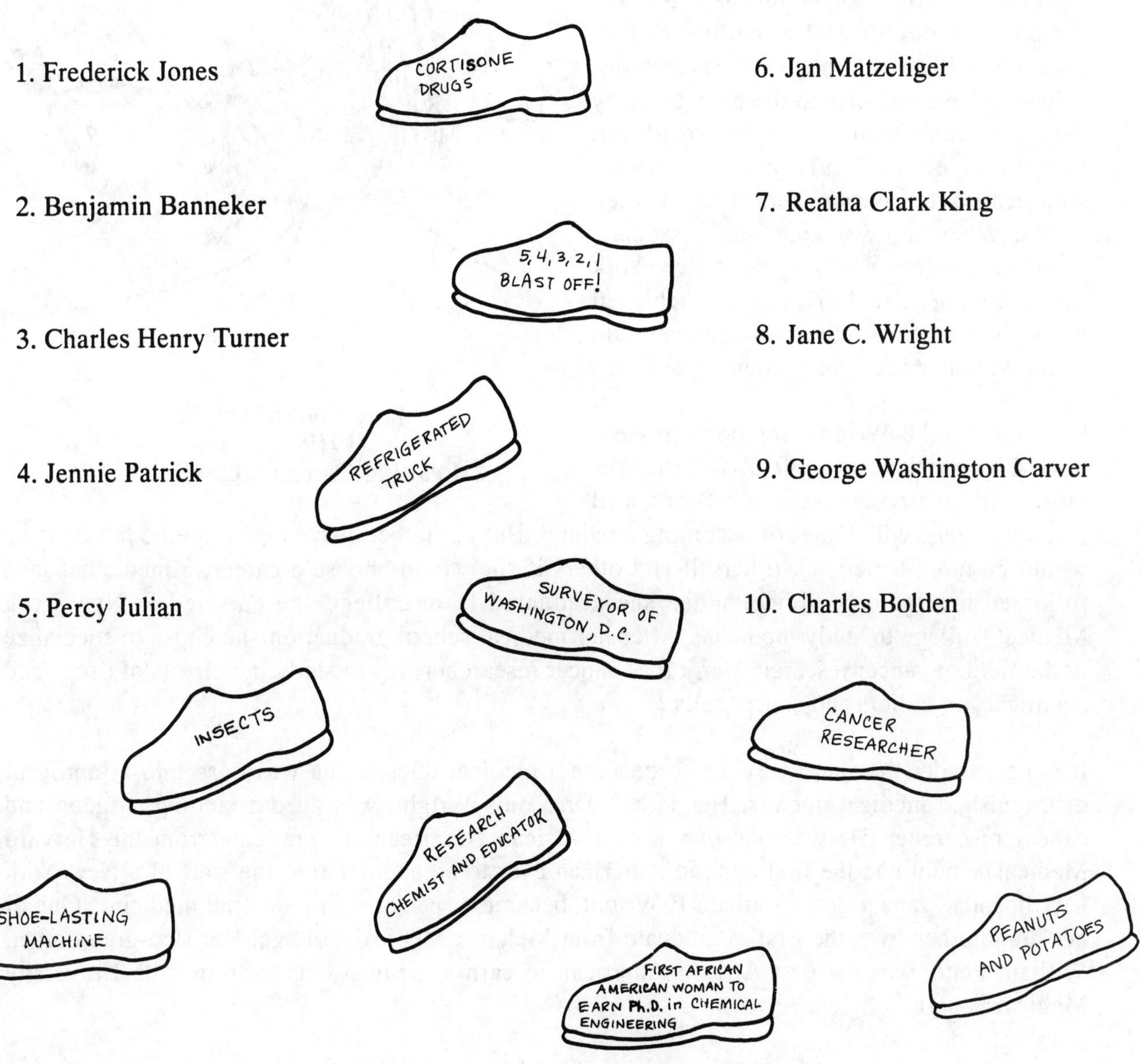

Jane Cooke Wright

Jane Cooke Wright
(1919-   )
Leading Cancer Researcher

To the average person, the word *cancer* is one of the most dreaded words in the world because it brings thoughts of pain, surgery, radiation and chemotherapy treatments, hair loss, and sometimes death. But to Jane C. Wright, the word *cancer* means fight! Dr. Wright is a doctor and a leading cancer researcher. Her work in cancer research has helped to save and extend the lives of many cancer patients throughout the world. Dr. Wright is one of only a few African American doctor-researchers in the United States. When she was appointed Associate Dean and Professor of Surgery at New York Medical College in 1967, she had achieved the highest administrative position ever held by an African American woman physician.

Dr. Jane Cooke Wright was born in New York City on November 30, 1919. She was educated in private schools there and entered college with hopes of becoming a painter. But her father discouraged her; he felt that she would be more beneficial to herself and others if she would choose a career in medicine. Jane followed her father's advice. When she graduated from college she enrolled in New York Medical College to study medicine. After her medical school graduation she chose to specialize in the field of cancer research. Her job as cancer researcher was to study the effects of drugs and chemicals on tumors and cancer cells.

It is no wonder that Jane grew up to become a medical doctor. She was born into a family of distinguished medical doctors. Her father, Dr. Louis Wright, was an outstanding surgeon and cancer researcher. He was one of the first African Americans to graduate from the Harvard Medical School and the first African American ever to be appointed to the staff of a New York City hospital. Jane's sister, Barbara P. Wright, became a specialist in industrial medicine. One of her grandfathers was the first to graduate from Meharry Medical College. Her step-grandfather, William Penn, was the first African American to earn a medical degree from Yale University Medical School.

When Jane's father died in 1952 she succeeded him as director of the Harlem Hospital Cancer Research Foundation and began her work in cancer research. In 1955 she joined the staff of the New York University Medical Center as director of cancer chemotherapy research. It was here that she did her greatest work in cancer research and became internationally known as a leader in this field. Dr. Jane Wright and her staff have not yet found a cure for cancer, but their research has done much to eliminate the pain and suffering caused by this devastating disease.

In Other Words

Dr. Jane C. Wright has been described by her colleagues as being exuberant, dynamic, determined, vivacious, inspirational, and insatiably curious.

Use a dictionary and write a definition for each of the following words:

1. exuberant: ______________________________

____

2. dynamic: ______________________________

____

3. determined: ______________________________

____

4. vivacious: ______________________________

____

5. inspirational: ______________________________

____

Use a thesaurus to find synonyms (words that have the same meaning) for each word. Write the synonyms opposite each word.

1. exuberant: ______________________________

2. dynamic: ______________________________

3. determined: ______________________________

4. vivacious: ______________________________

5. inspirational: ______________________________

Rewrite the sentence about Dr. Wright using some of the synonyms that you found.

____

____

Prevent It

Cancer research has found that cigarette smoke is the principal cause of lung cancer and that cigarette smoking also causes or helps to cause other cancers, including cancers of the mouth, pharynx, larynx, trachea, esophagus, pancreas, kidneys, and bladder. Many people have quit smoking; others have cut down on the number of cigarettes that they smoke.

Imagine that you have been selected by your principal to design three different posters to be posted in your school to warn students of the hazards of smoking. Draw a miniature version of each poster on the poster boards below.

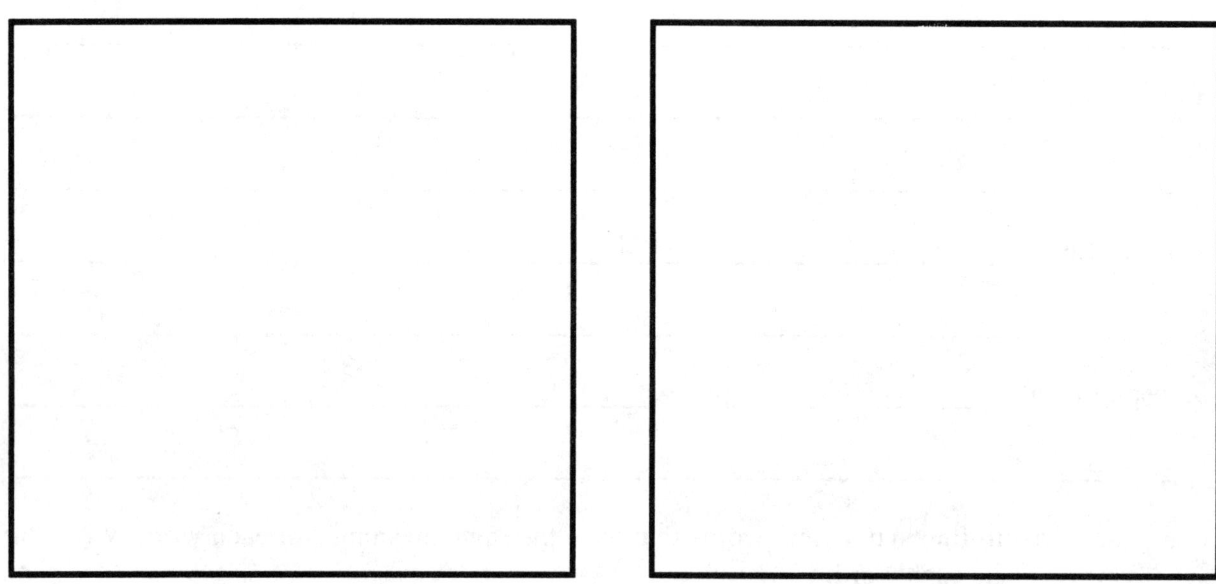

Twenty Letters

Dr. Jane Wright is just one of the many American doctors and medical researchers who has made outstanding contributions to the progress of modern medicine. The names of twenty others are listed below.

Select five names from the list and write one paragraph about each.

1. Theodore Lawless
2. Jonas Salk
3. Benjamin Spock
4. Charles Drew
5. Walter Reed
6. Benjamin Rush
7. Alexander Fleming
8. Daniel Hale Williams
9. Elizabeth Blackwell
10. Mary S. Calderone
11. John Gorrie
12. William Mayo
13. Percy Julian
14. Albert Sabin
15. Anna Shaw
16. Mary E. Walker
17. Karl Menniger
18. Alice Hamilton
19. Susan Picotte
20. Helen Taussig

Place an asterisk (*) beside the name of each African American doctor or medical researcher.

Medical Statistics

A disease is a sickness of the body or mind. It can be as mild as a common cold or as serious as cancer. Diseases have killed or crippled more people than all the wars ever fought. Each year in the United States diseases kill over 2 million people. Diseases are very costly too. In 1984 Americans spent over 550 million dollars on over-the-counter drugs to treat such mild diseases as colds and earaches. In that same year, colds caused people to miss about 26 million days from work and children to miss 26 million days from school.

How many days have you missed because of illness this school year?

How many days have each of your classmates missed because of illness this year? (Ask each student or ask your teacher to give you this information from her attendance reports.)

How many days have been missed by all the students in your school this year? (Ask your principal to help you with this information.)

Make a list of the different diseases that have caused students in your room to be absent from school this year. Choose one disease from your list and find out more about it. Use an encyclopedia or other reference book. If possible invite a doctor to your class to speak on a particular topic concerning diseases. If this is not possible, then use an encyclopedia and explore some medical topics on your own. Here are some topics that you might consider:

Communicable diseases

Infectious diseases

Bacterial diseases

Viral diseases

Noninfectious diseases

Nutritional diseases

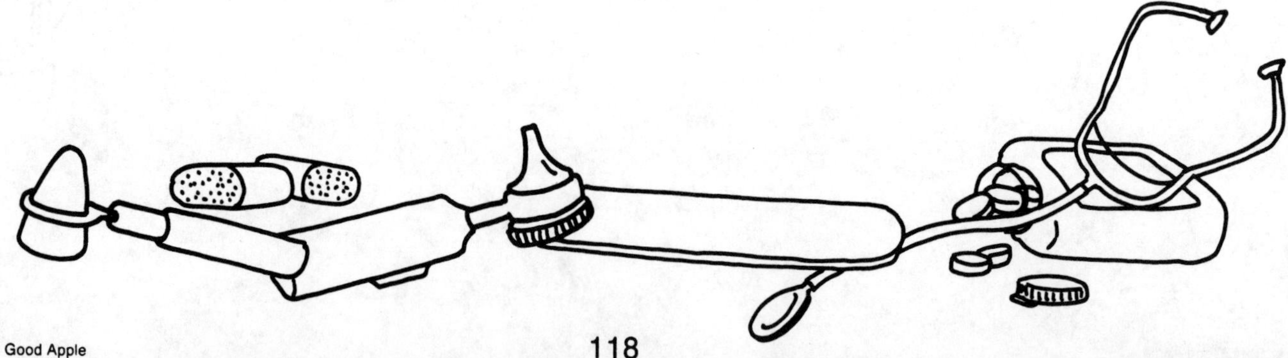

Joseph Lee

Joseph Lee
(1849-1905)
Inventor

Joseph Lee's first job as a boy was in a bakery. There he learned the art of making bread and the art of cooking. Lee liked his first job so much that he went on to make a career of preparing, cooking, and serving food. Later in his life he owned two restaurants in Boston, Massachusetts. In 1902 he started the Lee Catering Company which became a very prosperous business. During the summers, he owned and operated a fashionable resort that was known for its great fish dinners. In the years that followed, Lee became a master cook and inventor. On June 4, 1895, Lee was issued a patent for a bread-crumbling machine. This machine made it possible to produce large amounts of bread crumbs which were used in many different kinds of recipes. The Royal Worchester Bread Company in Boston, Massachusetts, became a big business, selling bread crumbs made by using Lee's machine.

Even though Lee received fame and money from his bread-crumbling invention, he went on to make another important invention. This time he invented a machine for mixing large amounts of dough. When bakers mix large amounts of dough together to make pies and cakes, the dough is heavy and hard to mix. Lee's dough machine made bread that had a finer texture and was softer.

Joseph Lee was a bread specialist, a businessman, and a restaurant owner. His inventions and businesses contributed much to the growth and development of the bread industry and the growth and development of Boston and the entire country.

Crumbling Cookbook

Look through cookbooks and find three recipes that use bread crumbs. Write them on the three recipe cards below.

(name of recipe)

(name of recipe)

(name of recipe)

When you have finished the recipe cards cut them out. Punch a hole in the end with the circle and tie them together with a piece of bright yarn. Display your recipes for a while, then tie all of the recipes from your classmates into a crumbling class cookbook.

Brainstorming Bread Crumbs

Brainstorming is an activity in which a person thinks of all the many different and unusual things about a particular subject. Try your brain on brainstorming. Think of all of the many different and unusual things that you could do with a cupful of bread crumbs. Try to think of original, clever, one-of-a-kind ideas. Silly ideas are okay too.

Use the back of this sheet if you need more room. When you have finished, place a star beside your most clever idea. Share your ideas with a classmate. Then make a "grand" list, combining all of the ideas from your classmates' lists. How many different ideas did you think of? How many different ideas did you and all of your classmates think of?

Making Dough

Joseph Lee invented a machine for mixing large amounts of bread dough. Play dough is used to make or mold things such as trees, houses, maps, animals, as well as other things.

Here is a recipe for making play dough. Ask your teacher or parent for help.

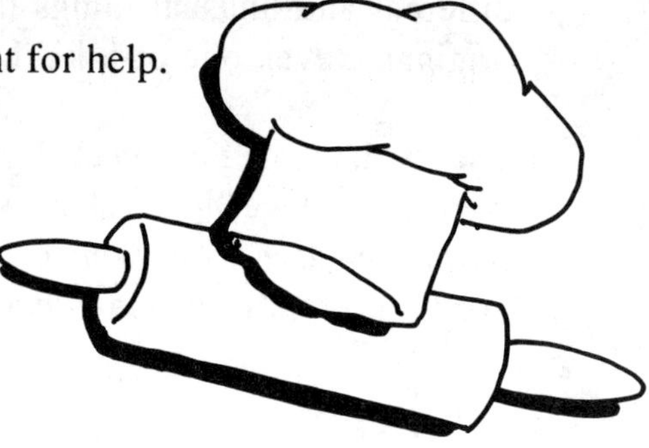

Materials:
2 cups (480 ml) flour
1 cup (240 ml) of salt
water and food coloring

Making Play Dough

Mix flour and salt together in a bowl. Add enough water to make a dough. Knead the dough by pushing and mashing it around in the bowl. Divide into equal parts for each color that you want to make. Add a few drops of food coloring to each part. Knead again. Keep adding food coloring until you get the color you want. Try mixing colors to make new and different colors.

Use your dough to make things that are found in a bakery, such as doughnuts, muffins, cakes, pies, and cookies.

To keep your dough soft and moist, store it in plastic bags that seal tightly. (Ziploc™ bags are good.) Put in refrigerator. Remove dough from refrigerator and let it warm up ten minutes before using it.

Invent a machine that will mass-produce sandwiches, pizza, tacos, or ice cream. Draw a detailed sketch of your machine, and tell the name of your invention.

At Your Service

In 1902 Joseph Lee started a catering service. A catering service provides food and services for a social gathering such as a Christmas or birthday party.

You are a caterer for a Thanksgiving dinner. What foods would you serve?

Appetizer: ____________________

Main course: ____________________

Vegetables: ____________________

Salad: ____________________

Dessert: ____________________

Design a catering truck or van for your catering service. Write your company motto or saying on the truck or van.

Write a television commercial advertising your catering service.

____

____

____

____

Walter Massey

Walter Massey
(1938-)
Director, National Science Foundation

Science and medicine both play a very important role in our lives. Research in these two areas has provided us with a longer life span and many other scientific and technological inventions that have caused dramatic changes in our life-styles today. There are many agencies that donate money to fund this kind of research. The National Science Foundation is one such agency. It was established in 1950 by Congress to help provide money for research in science and engineering. The NSF donates money to colleges, universities, and other research centers. When Walter Massey was growing up in Hattiesburg, Mississippi, he never dreamed that he would be picked to head an agency such as the National Science Foundation, but in 1991 it happened.

Massey was born in Hattiesburg in 1938. His father was a steelworker and his mother was a teacher. Both of his parents knew the value of a good education. They constantly reminded their son Walter that education was the key to success. Their steady influence on him caused him to think the same way. When he was in the tenth grade, it was discovered that he was a very bright child who needed more challenging classes and courses. At that time he skipped both the eleventh and twelfth grades and, without a high school diploma, he enrolled in Morehouse College in Atlanta. He graduated with honors from Morehouse in 1958 and went on to study at Washington University in St. Louis, Missouri, where he received both his master's and Ph.D. degrees in physics. There are very few people who earn advanced degrees in physics because it is such a challenging science that requires much studying and a lot of hard work. But for Walter this was not a problem.

After completing his degrees he held many important teaching and research jobs. At one time he supervised a research lab that employed more than 4000 people with a budget of over a quarter of a million dollars. Walter Massey has won many important medals, awards, and honors for his achievement in science and research. In 1975 he was named "one of the 100 most important educators in America."

For a black child who grew up in Mississippi, Walter Massey has come a long way. But Walter Massey took the shortcut–he stayed in school and got a good education.

#1 in Science

Walter Massey is the first African American to become the head of a major scientific agency such as the National Science Foundation. Before he became the National Science Foundation chief, he was president of the world's largest science organization. It was called the American Association for the Advancement in Science.

The year is 2500 A.D. You have just been appointed to head one of the agencies below. Select and research the agency and use the information to write an acceptance speech in the space below.

1. The Environmental Protection Agency
2. The National Wildlife Federation
3. The Nuclear Regulatory Commission
4. The National Aeronautics and Space Administration
5. The Tennessee Valley Authority

Crystal Ball

When Dr. Massey was growing up he loved to study math and science. When he grew older he began giving some serious thought to what he wanted to be when he became an adult. One thing that he knew was that he wanted a job in science or math.

Have you ever given serious thought to what kind of job that you would like to have when you become an adult? It's never too early to begin thinking about your life's work.

Several jobs are located in the crystal ball on the next page. Think about each job and place it in one of the three categories. Look up any job that you are not familiar with; then make your decision.

I definitely would not like this job.	Maybe I would like this job.	I definitely would like this job.
____________	____________	____________
____________	____________	____________
____________	____________	____________
____________	____________	____________
____________	____________	____________
____________	____________	____________
____________	____________	____________
____________		____________

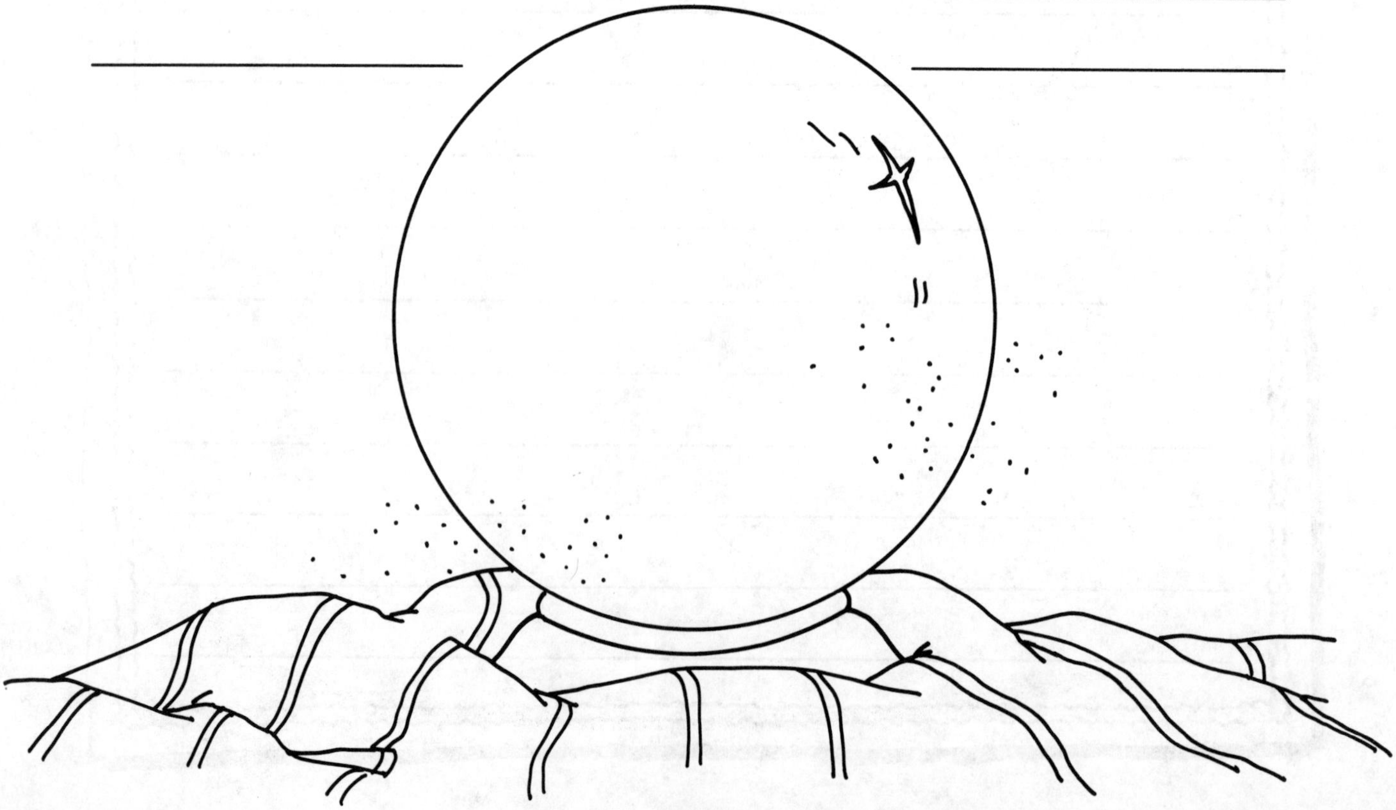

Job Crystal Ball

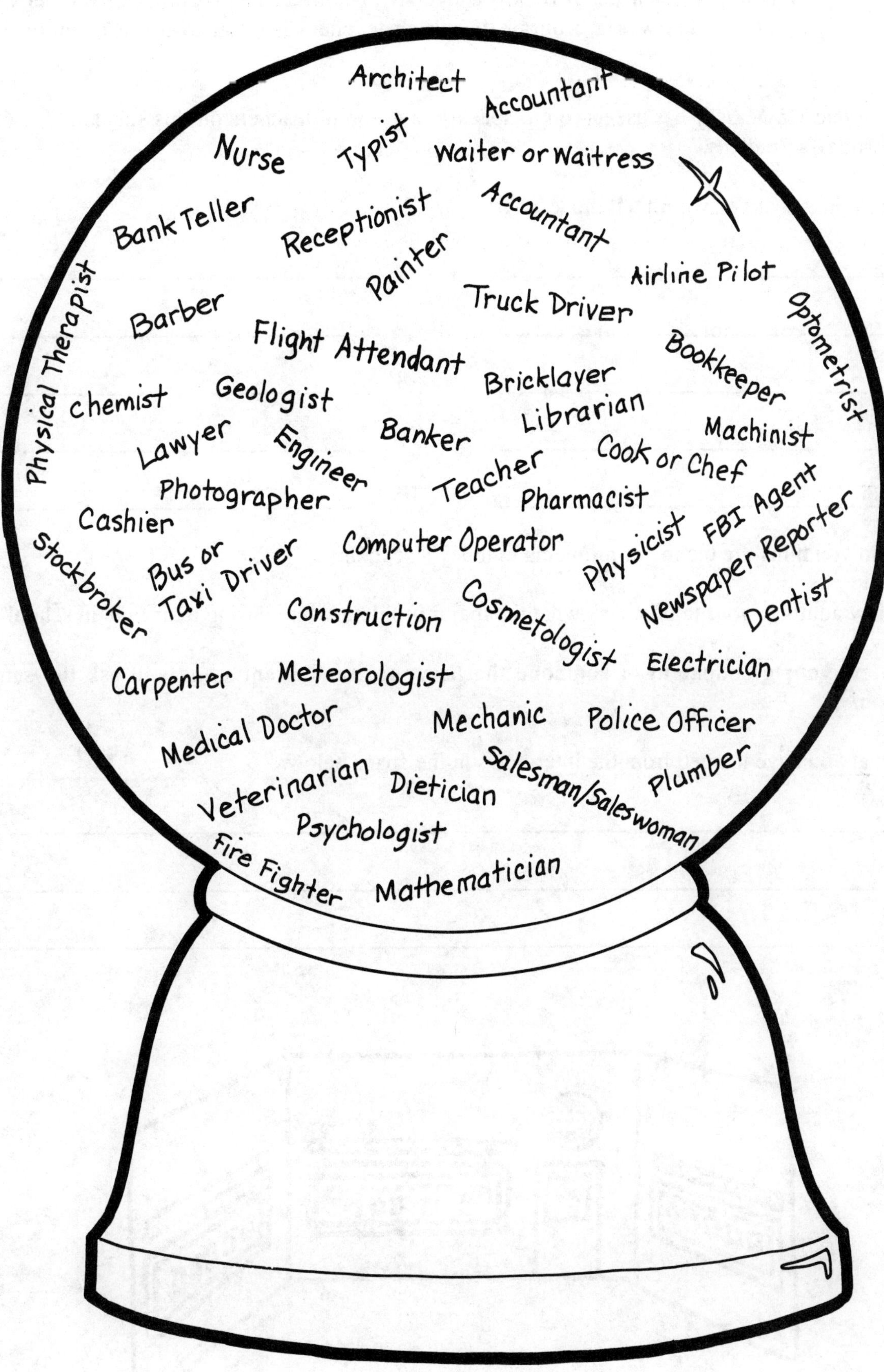

Ladies and Gentlemen

When Walter Massey was a teacher at Brown University, he directed a program called Inner City Teachers of Science. This was a program in which teachers learned to teach in inner-city schools.

Suppose that Dr. Massey has asked you to speak to a group of teachers on this subject: "How to Teach Today's Students."

List ten things that you would tell the teachers.

1. ______________________ 6. ______________________

2. ______________________ 7. ______________________

3. ______________________ 8. ______________________

4. ______________________ 9. ______________________

5. ______________________ 10. ______________________

What do you think are the major problems in today's schools?

Interview adults in your family. Ask what the major problems were during their time in school.

Interview your grandparent or someone that is your grandparent's age and ask the same question.

Tell what you have learned from the interviews in the space below.

____

____

____

Interest Collage

Many people base their career choices on their interests. Such was the case with Dr. Massey. Research has shown that people enjoy their jobs more if they are related to their interests.

Make an Interest Collage to show the kinds of things that interest you.

Look through magazines and/or catalogs. Cut out pictures of things that interest you. Paste them in the space below or on another sheet of paper in an arrangement that you like.

Use markers or crayons to color around the pictures to make your collage more interesting. Display your collage. Ask a friend if he or she can tell your interests by looking at your collage.

Invention Mix-Up

Below are the names of twenty inventors whose names are listed in the patent office. Unfortunately, the patent office is being repaired, and the names of the inventors and their products have been mixed up so that the office workers do not know who invented what. Can you help them straighten out the situation? Choose a word or phrase from the patent office that is associated with each inventor's product and place the word or phrase next to the inventor's name. When you have finished, circle the names of all the African American inventors.

1. Karl Benz ____________________
2. Louis Braille ____________________
3. Garrett Morgan ____________________
4. Alexander G. Bell ____________________
5. George Washington Carver ____________________
6. John Deere ____________________
7. George Eastman ____________________
8. Benjamin Banneker ____________________
9. Robert Fulton ____________________
10. Carlos Glidden ____________________
11. Robert Goddard ____________________
12. John Hammond ____________________
13. Jan Matzeliger ____________________
14. Johannes Gutenberg ____________________
15. Alfred Nobel ____________________
16. Samuel Morse ____________________
17. George Pullman ____________________
18. Isaac Singer ____________________
19. Linus Yale ____________________
20. Augustus Jackson ____________________

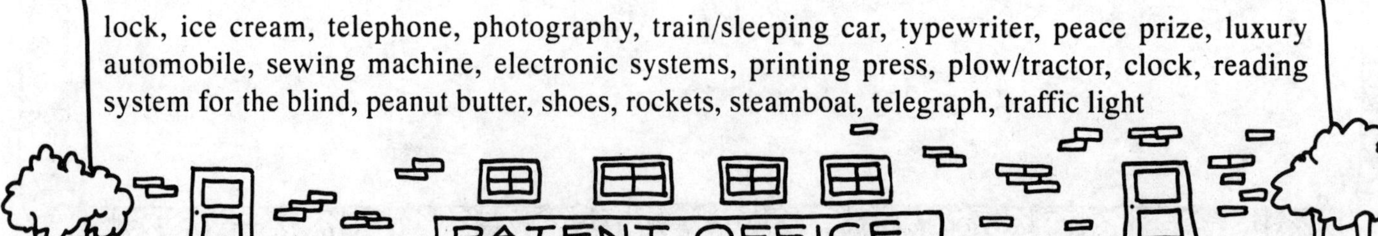

Map the Scientists

Find out where each African American listed below was born and place the number in the appropriate state.

Research to learn something else about each inventor.

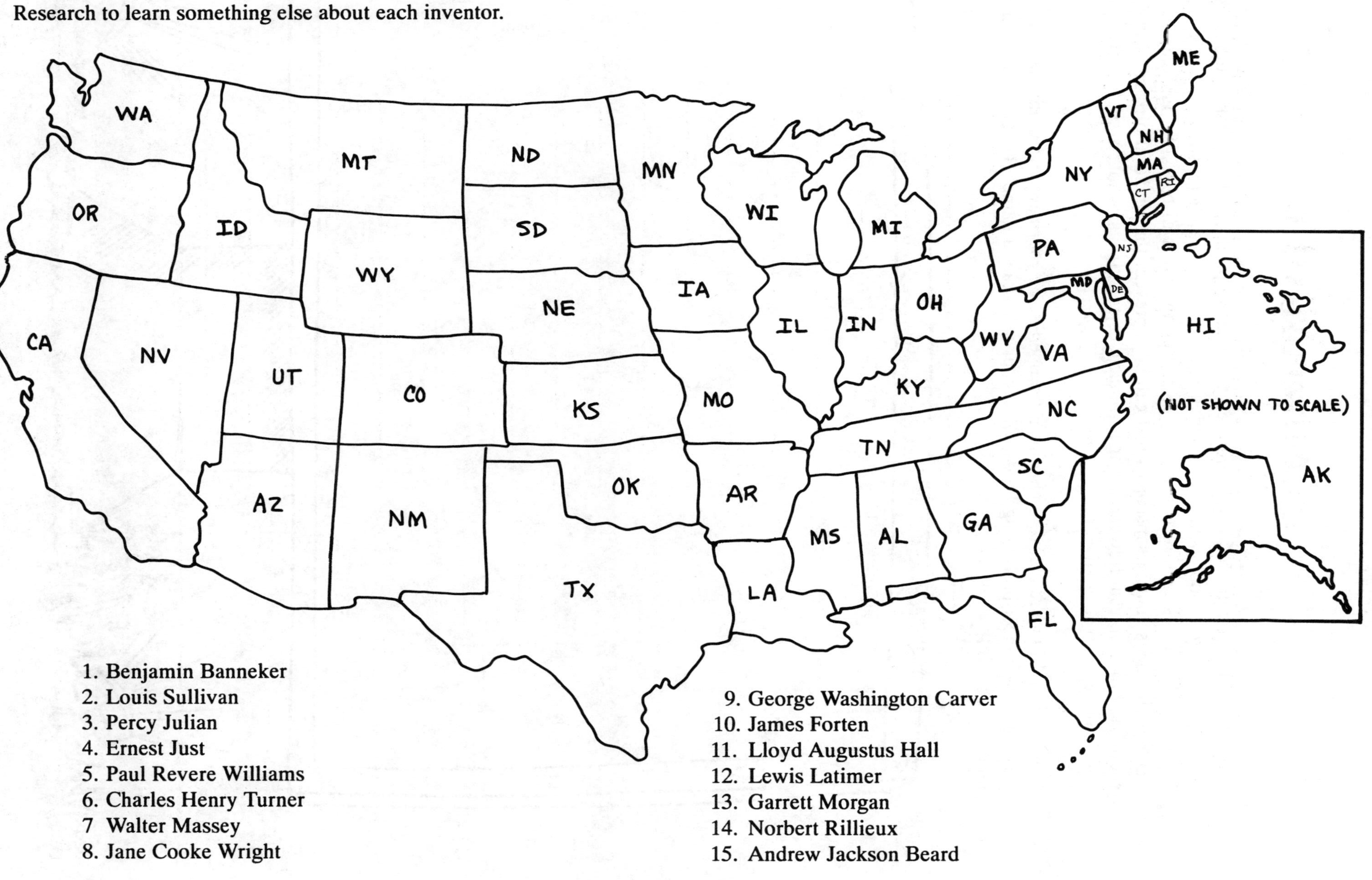

1. Benjamin Banneker
2. Louis Sullivan
3. Percy Julian
4. Ernest Just
5. Paul Revere Williams
6. Charles Henry Turner
7 Walter Massey
8. Jane Cooke Wright
9. George Washington Carver
10. James Forten
11. Lloyd Augustus Hall
12. Lewis Latimer
13. Garrett Morgan
14. Norbert Rillieux
15. Andrew Jackson Beard

Advertise It!

Throughout the country billboards are used to advertise products. How many billboards do you see on the way to school each day? Many scientists and researchers, such as African American Dr. Jane Wright, research to find out about cancer and other diseases. So far, they have found that certain foods contain substances that can help prevent this dreadful disease. Some of these foods are broccoli, cauliflower, cabbage, spinach, carrots, fruits, whole grain cereals and breads, and some types of seafood.

Use the mini billboard below to announce the opening of your new restaurant that specializes in serving these cancer-preventing foods. Give your restaurant a name. Be sure to list items on the menu on your billboard.

It's Magic

Amaze your family and friends with this simple science trick.

Materials:
transparent glass or cup; raisins; ginger ale, 7-Up™, Sprite™, or any clear, carbonated soft drink

What to Do:
Announce that you are going to hypnotize a raisin to make it obey your voice. Drop a raisin into the glass or cup of soft drink. The raisin will sink at first because of its weight. Then when soft drink bubbles collect on the raisin, it will rise to the top of the glass or cup. When the bubbles bring the raisin to the surface, they will burst and the raisin will sink again. Then bubbles will form on the raisin and the raisin will rise again. Just when the raisin begins to rise, say "Rise, raisin." When the bubbles burst, say "Sink, raisin." Practice your magic trick beforehand so you will know how long it takes for the raisin to rise and sink.

Try to "raise" other things such as sunflower seeds, peanut shells, etc.

Write your results below.

Evaporate It!

Do some liquids evaporate faster than others? Experiment to find out.

Materials:
aluminum foil
medicine dropper or drinking straw (Place the drinking straw in a liquid and place your finger over its top so it can serve as a medicine dropper.)
household liquids: a few drops of rubbing alcohol, water, vinegar, and oil

What to Do:
Put equal drops of the household liquids on a piece of aluminum foil about 2" (5 cm) apart. Observe for five days. Complete the chart to show evaporation results.

Put an *X* under the day that the liquid is all gone.

	Monday	**Tuesday**	**Wednesday**	**Thursday**	**Friday**
alcohol					
water					
vinegar					
oil					

Questions:
Which liquid evaporated the fastest? ______________

Which liquid evaporated the slowest? ______________

Try experimenting with other liquids and make a chart to show your results.

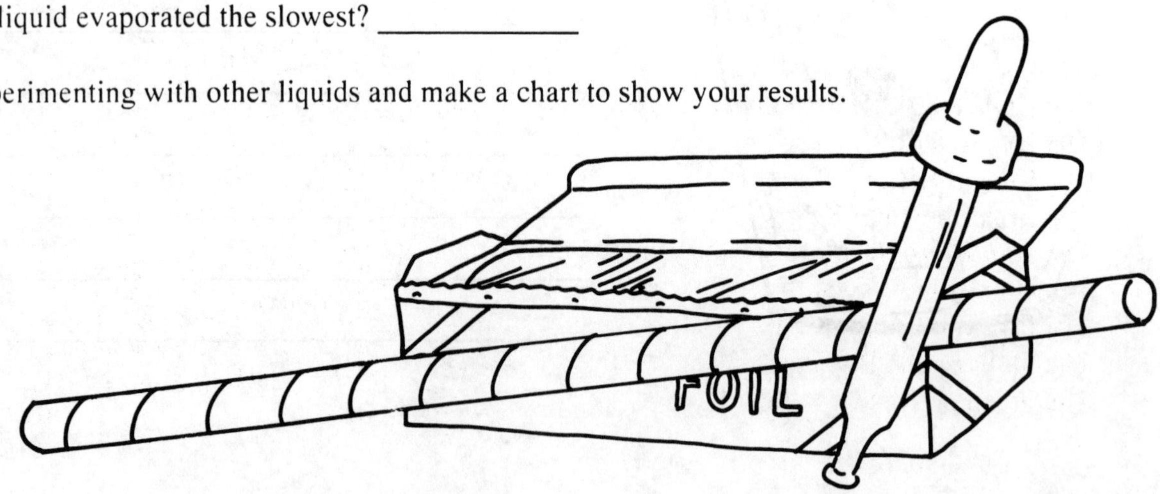

FOIL

Super Science Books and Kits

If you would like to read and learn more about science, here are some fun books and kits that can be found in many major book and school supply stores in America.

Books:

The Body Book by Sara Stein
Bugs, Bugs, Bugs by Beth Goodman
Computers, an Individual Learning Project by Doris Metcalf
Cut and Fold Paper Spaceships by Michael Grater
Earth Facts by Lynn Bresler
Earth Mysteries by Doris Metcalf
Ecology by Richard Spurgeon
Famous Firsts of Black Americans (Scientists) by Sibyl Hancock
Fifty Nifty Science Experiments by Lisa Melton and Eric Ladizinsky
How to Save the Planet by Billy Goodman
Inventions, Inventors and Ingenious Ideas by Time Line
Kid Stuff: People, Places, and Things to Know by Alice Siegel and Margo Basta
Let's Go Exploring by *Better Homes and Garden*
Mr. Wizard's Experiments for Young Scientists by Don Herbert
175 Science Experiments by Brenda Warpole
Outer Space-Fun Projects for Kids by *Better Homes and Garden*
Pond Life by Barbara Taylor
Rocks and Minerals by Doris Metcalf
The Science Book of Energy by Neil Ardley
The Space Atlas by Heather Couper
Thinking Upside Down by Doris Metcalf
The Ultimate Fun Book by Martin Handford
You Can't Believe Your Eyes by Crystal Tytla
The Young Astronomer by Shelia Snowden
The Young Naturalist by Andrew Mitchell

Kits:

The Ant Rancher Handbook and Kit
The Bones and Skeleton Kit
The Crystal Kit
The Environmental Kit
Fun with Hieroglyphics by Katherine Roehrig
The Gem Hunter's Kit
The Pyramid Explorer Kit
The Stethoscope Book and Kit
The Weather Tracker Kit

Great Scientists of the 1990s

Each year many large corporations select outstanding African American scientists to appear on their poster series. The posters are then made available to schools and other institutions throughout the United States.

Some of the scientists that appeared on posters in the early 1990s are listed below.

Read through the information about each scientist and complete the activities at the end of this sheet.

Dr. Jewel Cobb (Born 1924), Cell Physiologist
Dr. La Salle Leffall (Born 1930), Cancer Surgeon and Medical Educator
Dr. David Blackwell (Born 1919), Mathematician
Dr. Jane Wright (Born 1919), Cancer Researcher and Surgeon
Dr. Augusta White III (Born 1936), Physician and College Professor
Dr. Shirley Jackson (Born 1946), Physicist and the First African American Woman to Earn a Doctorate Degree from MIT
Dr. Jennie R. Patrick (Born 1949), Engineer and the First African American Woman to Earn a Doctorate Degree in Chemical Engineering
Dr. Lloyd Ferguson (Born 1918), Chemist, Professor, and Researcher
Dr. Reatha Clark King (Born 1938), Research Chemist and Educator
Dr. W. Montague Cobb (Born 1904), Professor and Anatomist. Taught at Howard University Medical School for fifty-one years.
Dr. Louis Sullivan (Born 1933), Former Secretary of Health and Human Services in President George Bush's Cabinet
Dr. Walter Massey (Born 1938), Professor of Physics and Researcher

1. Arrange the names of the scientists in chronological order from the oldest to the youngest on the time line below.

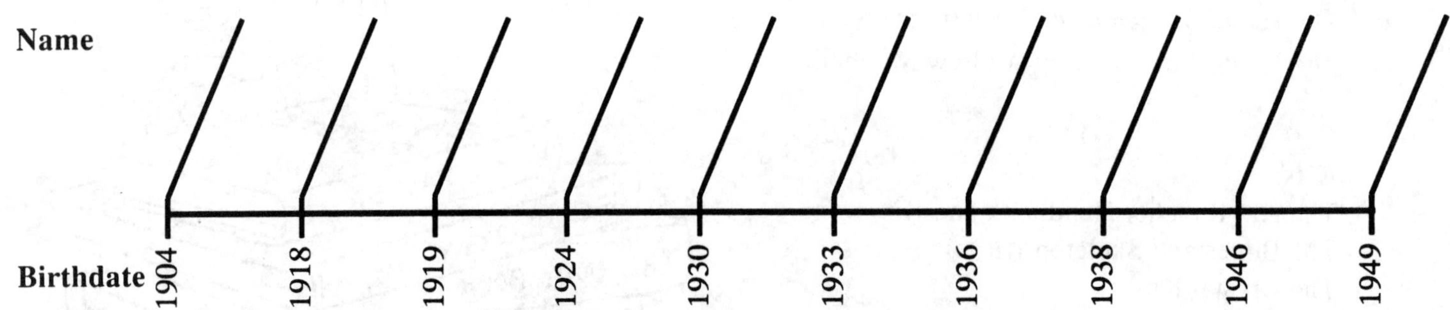

2. Use the "Great Scientists" information to make a true-false quiz. Test your classmates with your quiz.

Motion Picture

Motion pictures provide one of the world's most popular forms of entertainment. The movies have become a gigantic industry employing millions of people.

Many early inventions gave rise to the invention of the motion picture. One of these was called a *thaumatrope*. You can invent a thaumatrope of your own by following the directions below.

1. Think of a picture with an image such as a man bending over to pick up a stool.
2. Fold an index card in half. Draw the man standing up on one side of the card. Then draw the man bending down on the other side of the card.
3. Staple the folded card onto a straw like this:

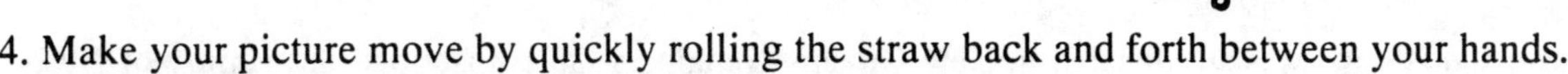

4. Make your picture move by quickly rolling the straw back and forth between your hands.
5. Try other images and make several other "moving pictures."

Research the history and beginning of motion pictures. Write your information below.

Sidney Poitier was the first African American motion picture actor to win an Academy Award. Research and write five sentences about this famous actor.

Historic Landmarks of African American Scientists and Inventors

Alabama
Tuskegee University: Burial place and museum of the famed Dr. George Washington Carver. The museum houses Carver's plants, minerals, and bird collection. Includes exhibits of various products developed by Dr. Carver as well as his paintings and research papers.

Illinois
Provident Hospital at Vincennes Avenue and 51st Street in Chicago. The first training school for black nurses in the United States was founded by the famous African American surgeon, Dr. Daniel Hale Williams.

Kansas
The George Washington Carver marker along Route K-96 in Ness County, Kansas, marks the plot of land farmed by Dr. George Washington Carver. He spent two years there working before going to college in Iowa.

Louisiana
The Louisiana State Museum located in New Orleans contains a tablet inscribed in memory of Norbert Rillieux, the African American inventor of the evaporating pan which revolutionized the sugar industry by reducing labor costs, thus lowering the price of sugar.

Maryland
In Baltimore, on Westchester Avenue at Westchester School, stands a marker in honor of Benjamin Banneker, the brilliant African American mathematician, astronomer, and inventor of the clock who published an accurate almanac in 1792 and led a survey team in planning the nation's capital at Washington, D.C.

Massachusetts
Lynn, Massachusetts, is the home of the famous inventor Jan Matzeliger whose shoe-lasting machine revolutionized the shoe industry by making shoe production easier and less expensive. The Matzeliger statue marks the home of this successful inventor.

The Nantucket Whaling Museum is on Nantucket Island, the hometown of Peter Green, an African American sailor. The museum features a treasury of stories and tales of African Americans who participated in the whaling industry.

Missouri
The Carver National Monument is a park in Diamond Grove, Missouri. It honors the great African American scientist Dr. George Washington Carver. The monument is the first ever to be created to honor an African American. It contains a statue of Dr. Carver as a boy and trails where Dr. Carver gathered and studied his plants. The park also contains a visitor's center and museum displaying discoveries and personal belongings of Dr. Carver.

New Mexico
In the spring of 1925, George Majunkin, an African American cowhand, discovered an archaeological find of bone fragments and spear tips near Folsom, New Mexico.

California
The plush and elegant Beverly-Wilshire Hotel in Beverly Hills stands as a monument to Paul Revere Williams, the brilliant African American architect who designed it. Paul Williams received the Spingarn Medal in 1953 for his outstanding contribution to the field of architecture.

New York
African American Vertner Woodson Tandy designed the Villa Lewaro. The Villa Lewaro is the home of the successful cosmetic manufacturer Madam C.J. Walker (Sarah Breedlove). It was declared a National Historic Landmark on May 11, 1976.

Answer Key

Cytologist, page 22

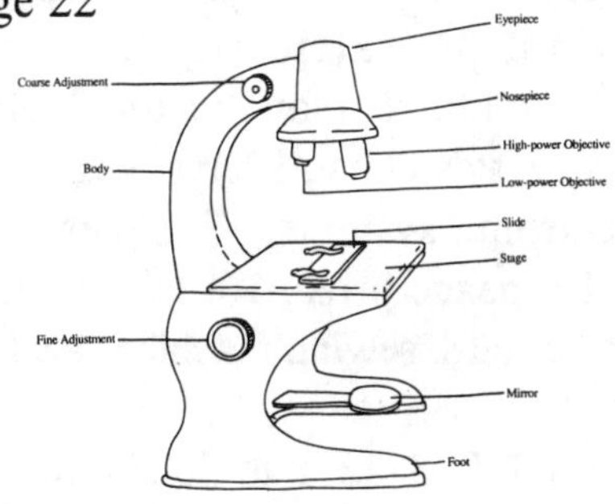

Symbolize It! page 27

1. H, 2. O, 3. He, 4. F, 5. Ni, 6. N, 7. Zn, 8. Ag, 9. Au, 10. Cu, 11. Al, 12. K, 13. Fe, 14. Na, 15. Ca, 16. C, 17. Hg, 18. Mg, 19. Si, 20. I

1. aluminum, 2. nickel, 3. calcium, 4. helium, 5. oxygen

Chemical Search, page 30

L P S S Q H W M H E E T Y C X U Y X R N C
C P K P Z M M K W T N U V F A M N T C A Q
E S X T S H V U W Z D I X M D T N F R S O
W N C C M F M R I S Q N D T P O E B H Z J
C U R O S U U W E C G R K O C W O O W Y T
R G H P P M I Q P I L O T I I N J Z R A G
S J W M R P S D N X U A L U M I N U M N L
N G G B L U E E O Q S I C D J T C X K T C
N V F N U N N R R S S I A N M R K K U F W
K E R H U I G E I F P I J B E O X C W Z Y
B N G R R Z A U P S K V L M H G Q K M R B
Z N Q O R Q M D N M R R E V K E Y U F D Z
B K U L R J R M H C U S M L E N F X Y E E
S L N A V D U F H T A I B S X R W T O S X
F Z E R S B Y V J C S B L M Q Q A P L S C
P Q U K R J J H L E E J X E U I B D C Z L
M Z A T C E Y E L O J V D E H I F X O Y R
S M I I I I P G B L R Q W X T B E Y P I D
L P U V U C N I Z N L Q S I U F Z O A U M

Space Maze, page 40

Whale Words, page 50

L R M N J H W O R W Z U D X N B N O N D J
W V Y N Y W T D L T D S A G U L E D A S W
N O I T A C O L O H C E E C Q D C E I F U
R T O L I P J L M L T L D K A B H B Q G A
X A Y A A R A N U N P O B O U W X Q S U P
Y D Y M K H W F P O X H U L O L M B L S J
F D I M C B X X U O G W I B U L F R A E V
Y P U A S E S I O P R O P N P E B X H I E
M T C M T Q N Q H R E L E Y S N W M W W L
N I J R E O P E Q A E B H T Q O U H R H A
Y J W A T N M Z E H N B U R R T K A A A H
B T C F Q W F V D L L L M O P K C C N L W
N K K J S A D R J A A U P R Y N A K D E E
R V C B G J B W C F N B B Q G A B B N S K
L I J A O K A K Q K D B A U M L N G V D N
W O D A C N A E C A T E C A Y P I C Q I I
M O G H L Y X X F C Y R K L D C F N Y U M
C U F G D C J F W W K X R S F G M B M Q V
W T P S Y W I E B H U R K F J L X B S S E

Categorize It, pages 58-59

1. barbed wire, plow, tractor, cotton gin
2. movies, radio, pencil, television
3. microwave oven, refrigerator, sewing machine, vacuum cleaner
4. microscope, thermometer, X ray, stethoscope, laser
5. laser, steam engine, telescope, electric motor
6. wheel, bicycle, airplane, automobile
7. dynamite, atomic bomb, radar, gunpowder

Invention Time Line, page 60

*Benjamin Banneker, 1753
Elias Howe, 1845
Walter Hunt, 1846
Joseph Gayetty, 1857
*Elijah McCoy, 1872
Alexander G. Bell, 1876
*Jan Matzeliger, 1883
Lee de Forest, 1888
*Phillip Downing, 1891
*George Washington Carver, 1900
Benjamin Holt, 1904
*Garrett Morgan, 1923

Have It Your Way, page 67
Russian–beef stroganoff, German–sauerkraut, Italian–pizza, Chinese–egg rolls, Mexican–tacos, English–Yorkshire pudding, Scandinavian–smorgasbord, Japanese–sukiyaki, American (USA)–fried chicken, Armenian–shish kebab

Objects of Communication, page 69
alarm clock, radio, breakfast bell, newspaper, phone, microwave oven, coffeepot, books, wall clock, car horn, traffic light, siren, tardy bell, chalk, pencil, hand, office buzzer, television, video, compact disc

Relationships, page 83
1. ink, 2. shampoo, 3. soap, 4. flour, 5. candy, 6. coffee, 7. cosmetics, 8. paint, 9. milk, 10. butter, 11. vinegar, 12. salad, 13. starch, 14. marble, 15. dye

Star Completion, page 97
1. star, 2. hydrogen, 3. helium, 4. times, 5. crops, 6. directions, 7. constellations, 8. planets, 9. revolving, 10. galaxies, 11. telescope, 12. supergiants, 13. neutrons, 14. sun, 15. light-year, 16. astronomy, 17. dippers, 18. animals, 19. mythological, 20. Orion

Insect "Myth"ology, page 105
1. T, 2. T, 3. M, 4. T, 5. T, 6. M, 7. T, 8. T, 9. T, 10. T, 11. M, 12. T

Other "Ologies," page 106
1. ornithology, 2. ichthyology, 3. zoology, 4. biology, 5. ecology, 6. herpetology, 7. bryology, 8. graminology, 9. mycology, 10. physiology, 11. meteorology, 12. bacteriology, 13. microbiology, 14. cytology, 15. virology, 16. embryology, 17. paleontology, 18. histology, 19. archaeology, 20. geology

The Shoe Is on the Right Foot, page 113
1. refrigerated truck; 2. surveyor of Washington, D.C.; 3. insects; 4. first African American woman to earn Ph.D. in chemical engineering; 5. cortisone drugs; 6. shoe-lasting machine; 7. research chemist and educator; 8. cancer research; 9. peanuts and potatoes; 10. 5, 4, 3, 2, 1, blast off!

Invention Mix-Up, page 130
1. luxury automobile, 2. reading system for the blind, 3. traffic light, 4. telephone, 5. peanut butter, 6. plow/tractor, 7. photography, 8. clock, 9. steamboat, 10. typewriter, 11. rockets, 12. electronic systems, 13. shoes, 14. printing press, 15. peace prize, 16. telegraph, 17. train/sleeping car, 18. sewing machine, 19. lock, 20. ice cream.
Numbers 3, 5, 8, 13, and 20 should be circled.

Map the Scientists, page 131
1. Baltimore, Maryland; 2. Atlanta, Georgia; 3. Montgomery, Alabama; 4. Charleston, South Carolina; 5. Los Angeles, California; 6. Cincinnati, Ohio; 7. Hattiesburg, Mississippi; 8. New York, New York; 9. Diamond Grove, Missouri; 10. Philadelphia, Pennsylvania; 11. Elgin, Illinois; 12. Chelsea, Massachusetts; 13. Paris, Kentucky; 14. New Orleans, Louisiana; 15. Birmingham, Alabama